A Wiser Woman on a Narrow Boat

Stephanie Green

Published in 2019 by FeedARead.com Publishing

Copyright © Stephanie Green.

A CIP catalogue record for this title is available from the British Libr

To Francoise, Jane, Sally and Seetha. With thanks for all your help (and the food and wine.)

Cover design: *marc@studiomarc.co.uk*

Contents

Part One – Setting Out

Dropping the Anchor

I'm having a long telephone conversation with a friend. She is having problems with her neighbours and it is upsetting her. I sigh and sympathise with her but obviously I don't sigh and sympathise enough.

'It's alright for you,' she says irritably, 'if you don't like your neighbours you can just drop your anchor and leave.'

She really doesn't understand the basics of boating.

Lifting the Anchor

I like my neighbours and even though I do have an anchor (it's a very useful large anchor; it just isn't attached to a rope or a chain which rather negates its intended use) I didn't really want to pull it up and move on. But as I keep saying, I have bought a boat that moves so I can explore the canal system of England. In which case I better, metaphorically, pull up my anchor and leave.

The winter had been long, cold and dark. I had cheerfully expected that my second winter on board a narrowboat could not possibly be as long, cold and dark as my first. It could be and it was but I coped with it better. I had got the hang of stoking the fire so that it stayed in all night and I got out of bed to a warm boat. I'd put thermal curtains over draughty doors and hatches, I'd looked up recipes for spicy soup and I'd kept my trusty hot water bottle by my side (or more often my feet) at all times. Winter moored on a riverbank has moments of great beauty, misty mornings, dramatic sunsets, ice on water and gently falling snow but I was glad when spring arrived. It was wonderful watching the river and the riverbank come alive. On the bank the trees and bushes sprouted pink blossom and green shoots and on the river ducklings and goslings scuttled after their mothers. It was invigorating feeling the dark nights receding and the days growing milder and as the wildlife and vegetation sprang to life then so did I.

I was living in a small water-borne community on the banks of the Nene and it was good to see people emerging from their boats and having an opportunity to stop and chat for a while without dying of hypothermia. I'd been planning to leave the river and set off for the canal system at the beginning of April but somehow April had gone and May had arrived before I finally decided that I could prevaricate no longer and I would have to go.

I awoke at 7pm on that morning at the beginning of May with a sense of foreboding and a thumping hangover. I could hear the wind and it was dark so I turned over, pulled the duvet up and thought that if the weather was bad I had an excuse for not moving. I'm a complete wimp about moving a narrowboat about on windy days; the slightest breeze, the faintest stirring of grass and willow trees and I stay firmly clamped to the bank until all is still. In reality I was looking for any excuse to stay put a bit longer and spend the bank holiday weekend chatting to the chickens and re-painting the little triangles on the bow of my boat.

Eventually I crawled out of bed and discovered the darkness was not due to bad weather but was caused by Bob's boat moored alongside mine. We, along with various crew members, were planning on travelling together along most of The Nene. As I winced into the daylight I discovered it was actually a beautiful morning. Bright sunshine illuminated the debris from last night's farewell party. I started a desultory clear up.

A few minutes later another bit of debris from the previous night's party turned up; The Man Who Knows Everything arrived carrying a holdall and heavy working boots. He dumped them on my boat announcing 'I'm sleeping on your boat tonight; I can't get to sleep on Bob's boat he snores and farts all night.' I wonder why he assumes that I don't snore and fart all night; probably this is because I'm a woman and in the gospel according to The Man Who Knows Everything there are certain things women don't do: snoring, farting, anything mechanical, play pool, hold intelligent conversations and think logically. He tells me we're going to overnight at Rushden and Diamonds where I'll be able to get up early and go to the big car boot sale, because 'all women like car boot sales.' Not much point in disagreeing, if The Man Who Knows Everything says 'all women like car boot sales' then all women like car boot sales. I'll have to go to one sometime.

I continued with my half-hearted attempt to clear up. Judging by the empties on the bank side a lot of alcohol was consumed last night.

As more people came blinking into the sunshine I was told the plan for the journey. I will be travelling upriver accompanied by Bob's boat. The Man Who Knows Everything and Bill are crewing for us along with my daughter who is yet to arrive. We are to stop overnight at Rusden and go into the town for a curry and a pint, get up early on Sunday morning to go to the car boot sale, which I must be delighted about because all women like car boot sales, then onto Cogenhoe and an afternoon BBQ for somebody called Andy who is celebrating his 50th birthday.

Then I'm told Tolly is coming along as well, so with a crew of three men I can expect lots of advice on to how to handle my boat.

I wasn't sure how my daughter was going to cope with all this, when I'd spoken to her, on the previous Thursday, she'd seemed a bit down. I feel the news that we are likely to have two rather strange and probably inebriated men sleeping on-board and another boatload alongside may be more than she could cope with.

I picked up Clare in Peterborough and she was low spirited; we sat in the bow of my boat in the sunshine and had a long talk and some lunch and collected my herbs from the river bank and put them on the roof of the boat and sat down for another chat. Despite all the talking I hadn't got around to mentioning our traveling companions for I feared that would really send her spirits plummeting and she'd either get the next train back to London or jump in the river.

We had intended to leave at noon, but it was 1.30pm before Bob's boat was ready and the men had unloaded four large boxes of Stella onto my boat and then proceeded to remove all the edibles from my fridge so that it could accommodate the lager. Due to all the sitting down and chatting with my daughter I hadn't yet had the diesel tank filled or the sewage tank emptied. I moved the boat over to the next pontoon to get this done, which delayed our leaving even further and gave Bill something to moan about. That

5

made Bill happy, Bill is only happy when he has something to moan about.

So at last we were ready for the journey, I could prevaricate no longer. There were two boats, three ageing lager louts, one affable young man of limited conversation and dubious hygiene habits, one daughter, a dog with a puzzled frown, an awful lot of lager and me all travelling together on this sunny May bank holiday weekend. Oh, what fun we will have!

Clare took one look at our fellow travelling companions and promptly put herself to bed in the hope that a few hours of sleep would give her the strength to cope with the rest of the day. Bob passed me a can of cider. The Man Who Knows Everything came on-board my boat and we were off.

It was good to be back on a moving boat. I worked out that it was over eight months since I'd travelled more than a couple of miles. It was a glorious day and The Man Who Knows Everything and I chatted happily about how fantastic the countryside looked in late spring. The banks were lined with hawthorn and the sweet scent of the blossom filled the air. In the breeze the petals drifted like snow across the river; the right kind of snow gentle, fragrant and warm not that nasty cold stuff that had been falling on us all winter.

After Wadenhoe Clare emerged refreshed and ready to meet all the eventualities of the journey.

We continued upriver. The alcohol consumption of the men seemed to equate to two bottles a mile. Clare sat in the bow reading. The Man Who Knows Everything was telling the story about how, when he first came to live on the river, he found the smell overpowering. Being a townie he thought that country living was all about nasty smells and he'd just have to get used to it. Then a neighbour came over and said 'Bloody hell what's that smell?' so they both looked around and found a dead sheep trapped under the boat. It had been there a while and had swollen to twice its original size. The neighbour got out his boat hook and prodded at it to try and release the body but only succeeded in puncturing it, releasing a cloud of noxious gas. The pair of them rushed to the bushes and threw up. The smell permeated the boat and surrounding area for weeks.

The Man Who Knows Everything's volume level was increasing in direct relationship to the amount of lager imbibed and he was switching into argumentative mode. At the next lock I tried to scrape him off but only succeeded in bumping Bob's boat. I wanted to exchange crew members, I was happy to exchange him for either Bill or Tolly although I would have preferred to exchange him for the dog. At least Max was sober and non-argumentative. For some reason there was a lack of enthusiasm from Bob for any swaps and he was just happy for him and Max to crew his boat and I could take all three men. By the next lock, I'd upset The Man Who Knows Everything by threatening to push him into the river if he didn't shut up. He took umbrage and stalked off to Bob's boat and told Tolly to take his place on mine.

Peace descended, Clare opened the wine and joined us at the back of the boat and we glided along. The quiet May afternoon had started to cloud over and a chilly breeze was rising and we needed to put on sweaters to stay warm.

By the time we reached the next lock the lager had taken its toll on Tolly and he lost his usual impeccable boating skills. He was working completely out of sync. Bob and I stood at our helms and watched in puzzlement as Tolly tried to close open lock paddles before the lock had filled and then close the gates before both the boats had left the lock. The lager had taken its toll on The Man Who Knows Everything as well and he was being even more argumentative and issuing instructions which the rest of us were ignoring. Bill decided to jump ship and come on my boat as well leaving Bob with one quiet dog and one argumentative crew member.

Leaving the arguments at the lock behind us, the four of us sailed along peacefully. Bill was moaning about a fish that lived beneath his boat. It was a very large fish and in the early hours of the morning it turned and squirmed banging on the base of the boat. The banging woke his dog who started barking and that woke Bill. 'Fancy being woken at dawn every day by a frigging fish.'

At the next lock we left the gates open for a boat going downriver. As we proceeded upriver we heard a blast of a horn and saw somebody waving from a bridge, we decided that there was no reason for anybody to need to attract our attention and they probably weren't waving at us but we waved back out of politeness. Two bottles of Stella further it suddenly dawned on Bill that there might be a reason for somebody trying to attract our attention. Did

8

anybody have the lock keys? Tolly hadn't got them, I hadn't got them, Clare hadn't got them, Bill hadn't got them. We went through a re-enactment of the procedure at the lock, but by then the crew was too drunk to know what they were doing when they were doing it so there was little chance of them remembering their movements fifteen minutes later. Bill and Tolly said neither of them was responsible for opening the guillotine gate. Clare said she was reading her book. In the opinion of the crew it was my fault, I couldn't quite see why I was to blame as I'd stayed at the tiller discussing philosophy with Bob and hadn't been anywhere near the keys or the gate but I accepted full responsibility. It was easier than arguing.

At the next lock it was established that nobody had the keys, so Bill rang Alan who then had to drive miles to the previous lock, pick them up and then come over to give them to us. Thank goodness for sober, albeit rather hung-over, friends.

It was late evening by the time we moored up at Rushden. The Man Who Knows Everything was definitely not talking to me, which was a bonus. Tolly was happily drunk and magnanimous and offering to buy us all a Chinese take-away. We got off the boat and as the cold wind sliced through us Clare and I promptly got back on-board, stoked the fire, got out the wine, made some pasta and left the others to go up the hill to savour the heady delights of a night out in Rushden.

The following morning dawned bright and clear. I got up to make coffee. Tolly and The Man Who Knows Everything had gone to the car boot sale. I managed to fight all my gender conditioning and stayed on board. Just after 8.00am they came back looking no worse for wear than they did on their most sober days and we all set off for Cogenhoe. At Wellingborough we stopped at Tesco's to load up with more lager: yesterday's boxes only contained empties. I had contemplated putting the food back into my fridge but when I saw them coming back across the park carrying another four boxes of Stella I knew that was a waste of time. As we'd stopped Clare decided it was a chance for her to escape and get the train back to London from Wellingborough instead of Northampton, somehow, despite her travelling companions, her mood had lightened but darkened again rapidly when she reached the station and found out the cost of a single fare to London.

So off we went again, now it was just me and Tolly on board. From the stains on his chin I deducted that Tolly had eaten a chow mien the previous night. The stains stayed there until later in the day when the beer dribbling down his chin washed them away. He told me it was an interesting car boot sale. Evidently it had good tool stalls and he'd managed to buy a few tools. I was going to ask if they had any good tee-shirts on sale, but I don't suppose he looked at tee-shirts because he has two, in a fetching paint-stained black, whereas a man can never have enough adjustable spanners.

We travelled onwards and arrived at Cogenhoe where Bob found the party had started at 1pm and not 2.30pm and was well under way. When I tried to switch on my computer the inverter tripped. It was now my turn to have a hissy fit. I was totally fed up with my erratic electricity supply and of my frequent inability to use the fridge and the computer because the batteries weren't fully charged or the inverter was tripping. I by-passed the party and stomped off up the hill to the village to try and work off my angst. It took The Man Who Knows Everything, my usual mechanical saviour, and his hairdryer to find the fault and sort it out. So now he could patronize me, and tell me how useless women are he was talking to me again. I was pleased to have the battery problem cured only it puzzled me as to why he carried a hairdryer with him for only a couple of days away. He hasn't what could be called a thick head of hair. If he just jumped up and down a few times it would be sufficient to dry it. But I wasn't going to jeopardise our new-found truce by asking pertinent questions about his relationship with his hairdryer.

I was relieved that the fault hadn't been flat batteries. If after all that time with the engine running the batteries hadn't been well charged then I would have needed to replace them and that would have been expensive. Feeling more sociable I joined the others in the bar for a while but I left early and went to bed with the Sunday newspapers.

By 10am the next day, the men were all showered, breakfasted and ready to head back to Oundle. Bob's boat was turned and ready to head back downriver. The other three were travelling back in the car which had been left in the car park.

By 10.30am on the Bank Holiday Monday I was alone and, only a year behind schedule, I was heading towards the canals. My only companions were a line of curious black and white calves standing knee deep in buttercups and peering in at the window. The peace and quiet was wonderful and it was great to be alone on my boat once again. I realized how much I relished solitude and I got the maps out to plan the next stage of my journey. I calculated that I now had more than twenty locks ahead of me, including a flight of thirteen on the Northampton Arm, before I reached the Grand Union Canal.

Twenty locks by myself! Sod solitude. I rang a friend and asked him if he fancied a few days of boating.

Reaching the Canals

With a little help (actually a lot of help) from the friend, the remainder of the Nene and the Northampton flight were successfully negotiated. I was back on the canal system almost two years after I had left it and over a year after I had intended to be there. It is a different way of life for boats and boaters on the canals. The canals were built for narrowboats, albeit working boats laden with cargo not the copycat narrowboats built for living aboard or holidaying that now populate these waters. The vast majority of boats on the canals are for leisure although on this stretch of the Grand Union there are a few historic boats and boats carrying fuel and coal. There are also some trading boats: boats that trade in sweets, cheese, books and jewellery, boats where their inhabitants are trying to make enough money to enable them to live on the canals and enjoy their chosen lifestyle.

I was alone again; my crew member had gone back to a warm house that doesn't have to be moved through a flight of locks with stiff paddles but with the promise to meet up in Braunston in a week's time. We will go together up the Grand

Union canal towards Birmingham and somewhere else after that (itinerary yet to be decided).

My beloved 60ft narrowboat Rea might have been built for the canals and she might be at home here but I'm more ambiguous about leaving the rivers. I keep contrasting and comparing the canal system to the rivers. I love the openness of the rivers, the unpredictable flow of the water, the plethora of wild life and the absence of boat life. The shallow, flat water of the canals doesn't hold the same appeal. Some days I enjoy the busyness of the canals with boats passing by constantly or moored in front and behind me but sometimes I long for a bit of emptiness. I know I can find emptiness by mooring on a quieter part of the canal in the middle of nowhere, but at the moment I'm just at Gayton Junction readjusting to canal life alternatively liking and disliking having so many boats passing by on the water side and dogs and their owners and walkers strolling along the towpath and peering in my window.

Yet there are things I do love about the canals, the ease of mooring being one of them. On rivers, suitable moorings can be few and far between and then, on EA (Environmental Agency) sites, the stoppage time is usually forty-eight hours. This means that journeys have to be planned, otherwise darkness can fall before a suitable place to stop can be found. Here on the canal system it is possible to tie up for fourteen days (except in some busy spots where the time allowed is shorter) and if an attractive place is spotted, or in my case an attractive pub, it's usually easy to just find somewhere to moor. If you don't like where you're moored move on, it is likely there will be another place around the corner. If you want to stop to stock the larder there is likely to be mooring rings outside the bank side of a Sainsbury or Tesco. As I have said canals are made for narrowboats but there are few fibre glass cruisers on the system. I have nothing against fibre glass cruisers, and I certainly wouldn't start using the derogatory terms plastic pigs or yoghurt pots about them, but I do worry about their vulnerability when I am around, especially when a strong wind is pushing me towards a moored line of boats or when I'm sharing a lock with one.

I walked down the canal towpath and then followed the route the horses took over the top of Blisworth tunnel. There is no towpath running through the tunnel and when it was first opened in 1805 the horses that pulled the boats were walked over the top of the tunnel while the boats were legged through. The men lay on the roof of the boat and pushed it through using their legs against the low roof or alternatively lay on boards placed across the roof of the boat and pushed against the side walls. In later years there was a steam barge that pulled the boats through but that still meant the horses got a short respite from pulling boats. The pathway over the top of the tunnel makes for a pleasant walk through woodlands, far preferable to being in that nasty dank, dark tunnel with the water dripping through the roof and the slimy weeds hanging down. I'm sure the hard-working horses of the bygone canal days enjoyed their boat-free stroll through these woods as much as I did. At the southern entrance to the tunnel the sheds that stabled the horses, if they arrived in Stoke

Bruerne before their boats, are now a glass work shop. The blacksmith's shop is still a blacksmith but making decorative ironwork instead of shoes for working horses.

If I needed to fall in love with the canal system instead of moaning about stagnant water, lack of wildlife and too many boats, a sunny Stoke Bruerne is a good place to do it. When it was originally built the canal spliced through the centre of the village and must have brought a lot of noise and busyness to a quiet Northamptonshire settlement. And like many of the new canals, and later the railways, it also enabled people to travel and to take their goods away from their own small local communities. Today the canal basin has been filled in, the corn mill is the canal museum and the brickworks are a nature reserve. Yet the thatched Boat Inn, the historic working boats tied up outside the museum, the Victorian terraced houses plus the informative notices still give the feel of what the canals were built for and what was achieved by visionary engineers and the hard-working canal builders of over two hundred and fifty years ago. It is great to sit close to the canal, have lunch and watch the narrowboats coming through the locks heading towards the tunnel knowing that, with a boat moored only a couple of miles away, I am a tiny part of this vast historical, re-vitalised, network of canals.

After two days at Gayton Junction I made my way in a leisurely manner towards Braunston and moored at Weedon for a couple of days in front of a boat that takes Brownies out for trips. Each evening an excited gaggle of Brownies got on board. From inside my boat it sounded as if an excessively

16

large and vocal flock of starlings had landed. Once they were safely stowed on board the boat set off and promptly slammed hard into the side of my boat sending me rocketing across the kitchen and spilling the cup of coffee I had just made. When I felt it was safe to let go of the edge of the kitchen cabinet I went outside to check for damage but couldn't find any evidence of additional bumps and bruises along my hull. When the boat returned it slammed into me again, luckily this time I was sitting down without a cup of coffee in my hand. The crew make such a dog's breakfast of mooring up that it was about half an hour before the Brownie pack could disembark. The following day the scenario was the same; an excited giggling, gaggle of Brownies descended, the boat left slamming into my side as it manoeuvred out of its space. An hour later it returned and slammed into me again before spending half an hour trying to get back into its long mooring space. I felt like popping out and giving the helmsman the names and telephone numbers of some good boat handling trainers and I do hope that Brown Owl and all those sweet chattering Brownies were insured against injuries.

I set off from Weedon on a bright and breezy morning ready for my meet up a few days later in Braunston. I reached Whilton, at the start of the Buckby flight, by noon. I wasn't looking forward to doing the Buckby flight single-handed, the locks are deep and the gates are heavy, especially the last one outside the New Inn where the lock beam is short and there are always spectators in the pub's bankside garden ready to enjoy the spectacle of a woman losing the battle with a large lump of wood. In addition, the old war wound of a knee injury was playing up. There are often volunteers helping boats through the first six locks of the Buckby flight so I was hopeful that help would be at hand. I moored up and went forth to check but there were no volunteers on duty that day. There was, however, a notice on the lock gate that said because of water shortages boats were asked to pair up to go through the locks. So that was my get out clause. I'm not a wimpy, single-handed woman boater hoping for another boat to come along to help me through the locks I'm a thoughtful, considerate boater who would much rather do the flight alone but is going to have to wait for another boat so I can do the environment a favour by saving water.

I walked back to my boat and stopped to ask the owner of a bright shiny tug style narrowboat if he was waiting to go through the lock.

'Are you by yourself?' he asked. I told him I was. 'You're limping.' He said accusingly. I admitted I was. He uummed and aahhed a bit and then told me his friends, who were travelling with him, might like a bit of lunch before they set off. I said that's OK I'll have some lunch as well, so he decided that I could take my time and enjoy a leisurely lunch and he'll just go through the flight with the next boat that came along. I could understand his point of view, he had told me that his boat was only six weeks old and he was taking it to the Crick Boat Show as an exhibit boat. He wouldn't have got any change from one hundred thousand pounds when he bought the boat and if I'd paid out that amount of money I wouldn't have wanted to take an immaculate boat through the locks with me. We agreed he'd go through the locks with the next boat that turned up and I would hang about for the one after that to come along. The next boat that came into view was a hire boat with eight young men aboard, all dressed as Vikings, on a stag weekend. Suddenly the new boat man decided that a lone woman with a limp was a better travelling companion than eight inebriated novices with crates of beer decorating the roof. I was a bit miffed. I'd rather hoped I could travel through the locks with the Vikings. My dream boat to share a flight of heavy locks with is one with a stag party of young men on-board. I don't care whether they are dressed as Vikings, Pirates or Elvis Presley (they're usually in the white satin jumpsuits of his hamburger years). I love their cheerful incompetence and the fact that with so many young men around I don't have to lift a finger all I have to do is stand there and give a bit of motherly advice.

But I did as I was told and prepared to go up the flight with the shiny boat. I went into the open lock first and passed my rope up to the friends of my companion boater who were operating the lock and waited for them to tie me up tightly. When I was secure the new boat gleamed its way in next to me. I was impressed with the perfect finish of the paintwork but I do find these replica tugs with their long flat bows and their abundance of large black rivets (stuck on rather than riveted) rather ugly. But each to their own, I think Rea is beautiful but this proud new owner probably thought she was a waste of steel.

All four of the people aboard the other boat were experienced boaters and our progress through the locks looked like being quick. As a bonus, because there were three people lock-wheeling, I was instructed to stay on board and not do a thing. Perfect. At the next lock the other helmsman was looking for every possible way of eliminating any potential scratch or scrape. He suggested I went through the pound, only a short stretch of water between the locks, in front and he would come alongside with his bow resting halfway along Rea and we would go in the lock together in this formation. I would keep hard to the left of the lock as I entered it. The scenario being implied, although not being said, was that I'd scrape myself along the wall of the lock and he would enter without any fear of touching the side or bumping me. I agreed and we entered the next lock, paired up as he suggested, and came in neatly without any damage to either us or the lock walls. We left that lock in the same formation but halfway along the pound for some reason he dropped back. I just went ahead into the lock, passed my rope up, tied-up and then looked back to see where he was. He was sitting in the middle of the low pound well and truly grounded. I suppressed my grin. He got his boat pole out, a brand new, unused, neatly painted boat pole, looked at it sadly and then reluctantly pushed it into the mud. He pushed and shoved for a while to no avail. The decision was made to let some more water down to try and fill the shallow pound. I remained in the lock, buffeted about by the torrent of water that gushed through when the top paddles were opened. When there was enough water in the pound to re-float him he came to join me in the lock. After that we reverted to Plan A. I went in first and tied up then he followed me in. We arrived at the top of the flight without a scratch to his perfect boat or to my imperfect one. He turned right and I went straight on, wishing each other a safe and pleasant journey.

I tied up just short of the Braunston tunnel. I hate tunnels and I needed a good night's sleep to physc myself up for the journey through this one.

The next day I donned my lifejacket, adjusted my headlight so that it pointed upwards to the roof of the tunnel, put on every light in the boat and went through the tunnel with gritted teeth and clenched buttocks. Yet despite my fears it was an uneventful passage; I didn't meet another boat; I didn't even hit the wall in the kinky part of the tunnel. On the other side of the tunnel I met up with another boater who was waiting for a companion to do the six locks on the Braunston flight. The boat crew were a young man and his mother who had brought two Downs Syndrome boys for a day out. As the mother's time was fully occupied in making sure the two boys didn't come to any harm in practice we were two single-handed boaters. We worked out our routine before we set off. I'd go ahead and open the locks, he'd stay behind and close them. The routine worked well. I actually felt happier than the day before on the Buckby flight because I was doing my fair share of the work. Although in theory I like others to do all the hard work I do feel a bit guilty about allowing it to happen.

We arrived in Braunston just after lunch. Rea was happy, she is Braunston registered boat and she had come home. I could feel her smiling.

A Contour Canal

The Oxford is a contour canal. My travelling companion tells me this at every tight bend. If he tells me this once again he will be admiring it's contours from a very wet viewpoint.

The canal builders of the eighteenth and nineteenth century had three choices when encountering a hill: go through it, go over it or go around it. The most expensive option was to tunnel under the hill, the next was to build locks to go over the hill and the cheapest option was to follow the contour of the hill and go around it. The advantage of both the tunnel and the contour canal is that they use less water than the locking system. That is what James Brindley decided to do in the mid 1700's (it was completed after his death by other engineers) when he designed the Oxford Canal. But the canal companies didn't build their canals for people like me who hate tunnels, are too lazy to be bothered with the locks but do enjoy the nice views offered by a leisurely, winding canal. The canals companies could never have envisaged that their canals would be used by us leisure boaters with all the time in the world to enjoy the view; on boats that didn't have space for cargo and weren't pulled by horses but had on board all the essentials of living in an age two hundred and fifty years in the future. The canals were built as a commercial enterprise and the speed of the transportation of goods was the prime consideration. From the old bargees' point of view dealing with hills by going through a tunnel was the quickest route followed by the harder work but efficient passage of locks going up and down the hills. These winding canals that followed the line of a contour around the hills took the longest to traverse. The expense of building tunnels had to be weighed against the benefits reaped from the subsequent revenue from the commercial traffic. As well as not envisaging the use of canals by leisure boaters neither did the canal pioneers envisage the advent of railways. The railways, that often run alongside the canals as they plough through valleys, carried freight so much faster than the most efficiently and expensively designed canal ever could. Not much more than a hundred years after the first canal was built, the advent of steam powered rail travel started gradually to compete with and make inroads into the profitability of the canal system.

The canal winds its way past the village of Napton on the Hill. The church tower on the hill remained to our left for a long time as we wriggled our way towards what used to be a tunnel at Fenny Compton. It has all the characteristics of a long narrow tunnel. It's just minus a roof.

It appears to be the unwritten law of the Oxford canal that you only ever meet a boat coming in the opposite direction when you are approaching a bend; the sharper the bend the longer is the boat that you meet. If the bend is sharp and also has a bridge across it then Oxford Canal law dictates that you shall meet a seventy-foot hire boat with a nervous crew who have only been on board for a few hours.

I took my first canal boat driving lesson along this bendy canal and was a gibbering wreck by the end of the day but since I've become more confident I enjoy all the reversing and negotiating around other boats and feel rather pleased with myself when we only have a few minor bumps (it was his fault!). I now have the confidence to increase power to get out of tight bends instead of slowing down and losing steering and if by a bit of skilful manoeuvring I avoid a collision I can smugly lean over and offer words of encouragement and advice to novices as they pass on by.

The Hatton Flight

We moor up outside the Cape of Good Hope pub and go for a walk before going in for a drink and meal. In the evening as dusk is gathering we go to have a look at the Hatton flight, the twenty-one locks that stretch up the Avon valley from Warwick towards Hatton, which we will tackle the next day.

We round the bend and steeply ahead of us is the flight of locks, there looks to be more than twenty-one, maybe C&RT (Canal and River Trust) have miscounted. It seems that tomorrow is going to be a day of hard work for whoever is opening and closing all these locks.

'I'm driving,' I tell Steve.

'Maybe we could share the driving,' he says.

'No. I drive, you do the locks. My boat: my choice.' I wait to see if he tells me where to put the boat or that he has suddenly remembered a prior engagement for which he has to return home. He doesn't say anything, just takes out his phone and rings his grandson, a strapping thirteen-year-old, and asks him if he would like a leisurely day out on a boat and promises him steak and chips in the evening when we moor up.

James arrives on this sunny Sunday in September on the Hatton flight, takes the news that he's helping with the locks with enthusiasm, after all there's only a few in front of us and then he can look forward to a leisurely cruise, steak and chips and I have promised him that he can have a turn at driving the boat.

He gets his instructions on how to operate the locks and we do the first five with the two crew members getting on board for the short journey between the locks and then we round the bend. Ahead of us, looking like a large white staircase, stretch the next sixteen locks.

James looks at the flight in amazement for a few minutes. 'Bloody Hell!' he says and then still open mouthed he looks around at his Granddad, the realisation that he has been conned sinking in slowly.

We stop for a quick lunch to re-invigorate the crew and in the hope that another boat might appear so we can share the work going through the double locks. After waiting a while then going back round the bend to peer down to the beginning of the flight and seeing there is still nobody else coming up we decide to go it alone. We take advantage of a boat coming down which has put the first few locks in our favour (this means the locks don't have to be emptied, we can just open the gates and drive in.)

Other boats may be in short supply but the walkers and watchers are thick along the tow-path and lock sides and I'm the side-show. What is the use of a canal without pretty boats on it? What is the use of trying to educate your kids about the workings of locks without a boat using the said lock to demonstrate how it has been designed? We have an audience, a following. Give me an audience and I can be relied upon to entertain them with my incompetence.

'She's never going to manage to get into the lock with only one gate open. Yes she is …… oohhh dear what a shame…….'

'Does it hurt boats when they scrape along the wall like that?'

'Is she meant to thump into the gate?'

One of my crew gets off leaving the windlass behind and I sling it over to him. It bounces back and lands in the canal. We get the sea magnet out and start fishing. For a while we only manage to catch either the boat or the metal piling. Spectators gather to see what we are doing. A toddler is getting perilously near the edge. If he falls in and is wearing old fashioned towelling nappies held together with large safety pins, there is a chance that we will be able to fish him out with the magnet. If he's wearing a disposable nappy, then he'll sink without trace. A windlass is suddenly fished out of the water. It's not my lost windlass that was painted a pretty pink (some joker thought that pink windlasses were appropriate for lone women boaters and gifted me it) but it will do.

We move into the first lock on the flight. Three children decide to help and try to open a lock gate before the lock has filled. They heave and push and push and heave and go purple in the face. Then the water equalises and gate suddenly swings open and they cheer because they have been strong enough to shift that nasty old gate.

A volunteer joins us and explains that although the instructions firmly state that the side paddles should be opened first and the gate paddles should not be opened until the lock is half full because otherwise strong flows are created that if there is only one boat in the lock then this advice can be ignored. He tells me to put the boat towards the back of the lock and he tells James to open the side paddle on the side the boat is sitting. The water then shoots out diagonally hits the far wall bounces back along the side of the boat and holds the boat in place along the side of the lock. Then the gate paddle on the other side of the lock can be opened and the strong gush of water from the gate continues to hold the boat in place in the lock. When the lock is half full the other paddles are opened and the lock fills quickly. Well I never knew that!

With James and the volunteer working the lock I am in and Steve going on ahead to set the next lock, progress becomes a lot quicker. James has now become an expert on all things to do with locks, boats and canals and is enjoying sharing his knowledge with the spectators, enjoying being part of the team that has a boat on the canal, forgetting how hard he has to work.

At the café towards the top of the flight four children stand at the edge of the canal eating ice-cream. I decide we all deserve an ice-cream too and I start to moor up to get one. I throw the centre rope to James and … 'F****k!!!!!

Don't be shocked dear children F***k is just a technical term we boaters use when we have miss thrown the rope and knocked our best china mug and the Nicholson's Guide into the canal.

At the last lock the crew are happy to have got twenty locks behind them and have in their sights the pub on the hill above. They become demob happy, get a new lease of life and have a paddle speed winding competition. First Steve's paddle is ahead and the boat slams into the lock wall on the left, then James gets ahead and the boat slams to the right. I shout succinct instructions at the winders which they ignore. Experienced boaters would say I should have tied up the boat when I was in the lock but we'd managed the last twenty locks without incident and I have a habit of getting my knots wrong and tying up too securely and feeling the boat keel over as the water comes up. The spectators gather and wince at each hefty slam of boat against lock wall. As the boat emerges from the depths they peer in the windows and I can tell from their expressions that it's not a pretty sight in there. When I go down to check my books and pictures are all scattered across the floor. The wall clock is spewing its innards over the worktop and the cupboard doors are open and their contents falling out.

We leave the lock, moor up, the crew wends their weary way towards the pub and I follow after I've restored the boat contents to their rightful places. I buy them both a drink but I'm not talking to them. My sulk goes unheeded as they are chatting happily to each other and not noticing me at all.

I get up the next morning and go out with the camera. It is early but men with strimmers are out, the buzz of the machines drowning the morning chorus of bird song. The rubbish left behind from a busy Sunday is being collected.

The area around Hatton is well kept and attractive. I love the picnic tables constructed from parts of old lock gates with yellow and grey lichen adding texture and colour to their surfaces. I love the seating, the backs made from the wooden pilings that once used to support the banks of the canals the seats from solid wood engraved with patterns. I'm standing at the top of the hill and can see the flight of locks glistening whitely as they stretch down towards Warwick. Here the old maintenance yards where once the lock gates where built are now restored and used as offices, here the old stable block for the horses that pulled the barges is now a café. In the hazy sunshine of an early morning the whole area is extremely pretty. There are the reminders of our industrial heritage in these buildings, and picnic tables, in the unused side locks which date from the late eighteenth century but were replaced by the wide concrete locks in the 1990's. The information plaques give interesting facts about the canal system and the stainless-steel statue of a dragonfly in a side pond is eye-catching.

The whole area is a reminder that nowadays the canals are not just for boaters in their nicely painted boats but for the cyclists and the walkers and the watchers (I dislike the word gongoozlers which the towpath walkers and watchers are often called). The canal system is the inheritance of everybody in this country and as such must be preserved. Boaters are instrumental in this preservation, by using the canals they are preserving them, but although they might pay more for being there they also demand more in the way of maintenance and facilities. I can moan with the best of them about the high salaries paid in the upper echelons of C&RT and don't get me started on the subject of fishermen but it is a difficult task keeping the interests of all the users of the canal system satisfied when the funding is diverse yet limited.

Towards Oxford

In Banbury the town moorings were full. Through the town lock and only a few hundred yards further on there were a long stretch of moorings that backed up to the industrial park. I didn't like the look of these, the area appeared seedy and I felt uncomfortable with it. As I hoped to stay in Banbury for a few days and I would be by myself I was a bit picky about where I moored the boat. I carried on and found a pleasant looking mooring at the end of a long line of boats, across from parkland and next to a quiet office development. Later that evening when I was chatting to the lady from one of the other boats I noticed a sign, half obscured by trees, saying that these were permanent moorings. 'That's OK,' she said, 'it's Bill's moorings and he's out for the summer and he doesn't mind friends of mine staying on his mooring.' Isn't that nice, all I did was help her turn her boat around so she could clean the other side, stroke her cat and talk about the weather and the price of fish in Morrisons and I'm her friend. It's so easy to make friends on the canals.

I had planned to make my way gradually to Oxford and the Thames. I was concerned about the swing bridges between Banbury and Oxford. I assumed that when the canal was first built these swing bridges, which are a feature of the Oxford Canal, were the most economical way of allowing farmers to move from field to field when the canal cut through their land. It would be far cheaper to put a flat, wooden bridge with a chain to pull it up than to build one of those pretty, arched brick bridges. The only problem is that, although many of the bridges are left open, the ones that are closed aren't easy for the single-handed boater to operate. They often aren't easy for the short-arsed and feeble either, many of the mechanisms being heavy and the chains to pull the bridges down not being very long. So being both single-handed and short arsed I was at a dual disadvantage. If the boat is tied up on the towpath side the boater has to cross the bridge to open it. Once the bridge is opened the boater is then stranded on the opposite side of the canal to the boat and with no way of getting back unless the bridge is lowered again or they swim (actually, as the canals aren't very deep they could just paddle). I'd strolled down the canal and worked out that there are three ways of managing these bridges. Either wait for another boat to come along, ask passing dog walkers to help or moor up on the non-towpath side with the bow of the boat poking under the bridge and then leap into the bushes. I'm not good at asking passers-by for help and I'm even worse at leaping off the boat without causing myself serious injury so I wasn't sure what to do. I was asking a couple of single-handed boaters who were moored at Banbury how they coped and one of them told me he was heading towards

Oxford the next day and if I didn't mind waiting around another day we could travel together.

We set off the following morning, a thin drizzle permeated all my clothing in about ten minutes. We set off without deciding on a system of getting us through the bridges. Our lack of communication meant that at the first bridge we almost stranded both of us on the wrong side of the canal. It was then decided that the routine would be for me to moor up first and open the bridge, he would drive through, tie-up and come back and drive my boat through. It was at this point I realised that this nice, young man on his shiny, black boat stuffed with music and recording equipment was actually doing me a big favour by travelling along this stretch of canal with me. He was perfectly capable of leaping onto distant banks and pulling his boat under bridges and to have to tie up to help a stiff, old lady along was adding to the time taken for his journey. Though, on the plus side he wouldn't have nasty scratches from the blackthorn bushes along the side of his beautiful paintwork. At the next bridge our system worked well and after that we met a boat travelling in the opposite direction, whose crew opened the bridge for us. But mostly the bridges were propped open so we didn't need a system.

I must have also held him up at the locks even though we worked through them quickly and efficiently. The locks on the Oxford canal are single locks and unlike double locks where there is an advantage having two boats travelling together there is little advantage in having two boats travelling through single locks. Also fit young men can scale ladders, jump across gates and hop onto their boats with great alacrity and pass through locks much more quickly than any middle-aged faffer can. Each single-handed boater has their own method of working (apart from me) and if I have shared locks with single-handed boaters I always ask what it is and then work with their preferred routine. Then I watch young men jump over spaces the size of the Grand Canyon, drop down onto the roofs of their boats miles down in the locks and wind stiff paddles with one hand while rolling a cigarette with the other. I just stand there and think, 'I wish I could do that.' When I am a single-handed boating, my preferred method is to either lurk near the lock until somebody else comes along or, failing that, hope that nobody is watching and I am not pressured into feeling the need to appear an experienced boater. That is when accidents happen, when I am rushing to appear quick and efficient although my natural way of working is slow and incompetent.

We reached Aynho Weir Lock. I thought it was a strange looking lock; it's large and diamond shaped and has a rise of only one foot. There must be a good reason for this odd-looking work of engineering. Maybe it's because from here onwards the Cherwell River crosses and then later joins the canal that there needs to be control over water levels. We spent a lot of time looking at it and trying to work out if our 60ft and 70ft boats would fit into it together before deciding they wouldn't. A wise decision as I think we'd still be jammed in that lock. Just as I was passing under Belchers Bridge I had a telephone call from a friend, a Mr Belcher. It was a strange co-incidence, the type I often think of as being serendipity or spooky but is really only a strange co-incidence. He asked if I was anywhere in the vicinity of Aynho as he was travelling home and had just crossed the canal. If I was nearby we could meet up in the pub. That seemed like a good idea. I let my travelling companion know I was stopping at Aynho. I think he was glad to see the back of me but he was far too polite and charming to let me know that and simply thanked me for my help (more hindrance than help methinks) and went on his way.

To Lechlade

I moored the boat at Kidlington for a week. It was an easy bus journey into Oxford and from Oxford a cheap and efficient bus service ran into London. I also made use of the cross-country X5 bus to Cambridge although it may have been quicker to walk there.

Steve joined me at Kidlington through a lock and a lift bridge and then make a right turn passing through the rather grimy Duke's Cut Lock onto the overgrown and gloomy Duke's Cut. The heavy vegetation opened suddenly onto the bright waters of the Thames with a view across the flat, green water meadows to Godstow. This is the quietest part of the navigable Thames. Quiet because many of the smarter, larger cruisers, the ones that justify the sobriquet of gin palaces, are too high to fit under the low Osney Bridge. At Eynsham Lock we had the first taste of a Thames lock, and I was impressed. The lock-side was immaculately kept and dense with flowers. The lock-keeper was friendly and helpful and as it was our first time at a Thames lock he patiently explained the protocol. The bow and stern ropes are to be wrapped around bollards. As the water flows in I will hold tight onto the stern rope and Steve will hold the bow rope. The theory was fine but the actuality went a bit adrift. The water came in faster and with more force than I expected, Steve pulled the bow in harder than I expected and I ended up competing with him so I could hold in the stern. Then the rope sprung from the bollard it was attached to (I should have had it on the far-side of the boat not the nearside!). I grabbed hold of the rope as it sprang upwards and was then holding on to both ends of it and my arms were nearly pulled out of their sockets. In the end I decided against acquiring serious strain injuries and I let the rope go. The stern bounced away from the wall. Luckily we were the only boat in the lock. The lock-keeper looked back, puzzled. 'Do you know what she's trying to do?' he asked Steve. Steve shrugged his shoulders and then they both nodded in a moment of male bonding, a silent agreement about the strange habits of women.

It was a fine early evening when we moored up beyond the lock on the meadows at Swinford, at the end of a long line of boats. An argument ensued. I can't even remember what the argument was about but it was obviously very serious because I threw all his possessions into the field and locked the doors on him. He put his belongings into his red rucksack and set off towards Swinford Bridge. As he disappeared I could see him nodding a 'Good Evening,' to the line of boaters, sitting out on the riverbank, as he walked past them. The red rucksack faded into the distance as he went on his way and then I saw it pass over the bridge. I had calmed down by then and remembered, as he disappeared from view, that the locks on the Thames appeared to be a two-man job, the ropes at the stern and rear needed to be attached and held. How was I going to manage by myself? I sent him a text saying, 'Come back home, all is forgiven.' About five minutes later I saw the red rucksack heading back over the bridge, then down the river bank, with its owner again nodding a 'Good evening,' to same boaters he'd spoken to on the half an hour earlier on his way back home.

After that the journey along the winding and idyllic Thames was harmonious, although a few months and a few trips later a terminal argument ensued. I ceremoniously dumped his walking boots in the River Nene and watched them bob away downstream, until they joined some of ducks by the weir and the brown boots merged with the brown plumage of the mallards and became one with the wildlife.

I had been warned that this twisty, sometimes narrow, sometimes overgrown section of the Thames could be difficult to negotiate. That there were many shoals that could ground an unwary boater, that there were sharp bends which were difficult to get around, that there were blind corners where oncoming boats were a collision hazard. Yet I enjoyed the small challenges of not grounding the boat and not getting her bow stuck on the bends and not causing death and destruction to fragile cruisers. The only time I went wrong was when there was a red marker buoy adrift in the centre of the river. It was a fifty/fifty choice on which route to take around the buoy and I chose the wrong fifty.

I think the highlight of my trip up the Thames (apart from just being there) was an opportunity to visit Kelmscott Manor the former home of William Morris. We reached

Kelmscott on one of the two days in the week it was open, an unusual occurrence: I usually reach places I want to visit on the one day they are closed. We got a place to moor along an uneven meadow and in we went. My son had done a project on William Morris for his 'A' level Art. I'd become involved so therefore I felt I'd done the project as well and was very familiar with the Arts and Crafts movement. Because Kelmscott Manor is closed in the winter (when all good school projects take place) we hadn't visited it. It didn't disappoint, it is a stunning building in a glorious setting. The interior shows the crafts, paintings and fabrics of the Arts and Crafts era in a calm and unfussy way. The middle-class lady volunteers are enthusiastic and knowledgeable. If it had been open when we went back down the Thames, I would have liked to visit it again but I wasn't lucky enough to be passing by twice on its limited opening days.

We moored at Lechlade for a couple of nights, against a cow field, a short walk into the town. I didn't take the boat down to the end of the navigation but we did walk down. Five girls were ignoring the signs that said 'Danger: do not jump from the Bridge' and were jumping from the bridge accompanied by much splashing and squealing. Three teenage boys standing on the bankside were horrified.

'Don't they know it's dangerous!', 'They should read the notices', 'They may be seriously injured', they muttered to each other. Then one got his phone out and the general consensus of opinion amongst them was that they should ring the police and report the girls. What has happened to the youth of today? It used to be sex, drugs and rebellion now it's all about health and safety and the reporting of misdemeanours to the authorities.

Then it was turn around, back down the Thames to Oxford for an equally idyllic and harmonious cruise. The only shock was the price of the meal when we over-indulged at the Trout Inn at Tadpole Bridge. I noticed there were another two Trout Inns along this stretch of the Thames (and one Perch Inn), when I asked a couple of fishermen if they ever caught any trout neither of them had.

I came back through Dukes Cut then into Oxford, happy to still have somebody to help with the lift bridges. After turning right into Oxford there is a long row of Agenda 21 moorings. Agenda 21 was a motion passed in a United Nations conference in Rio in 1992 and is a commitment to local communities and the environment. The moorings are now a collaboration between British Waterways and the Oxford Boaters Co-op. Basically they are reasonably priced moorings close to the city of Oxford. Cheap moorings near a city where residential property prices are high? It's a pity there aren't more places like that. Except cheap moorings have a price. When I noticed two boats for sale I also noticed that their asking price was about £30,000 more than one would expect for boats of that age and build. These sort after moorings are obviously for sale with the boat, this must negate the original intention of the boaters to have a reasonably priced and stable mooring. Some boats are smart and well-kept, others older but quirky and neat, some just make you doubt the owners 'commitment to local communities and the environment'.

41

As I bumbled slowly past the Agenda 21 moorings, peering in at windows, commenting on the boats, grumbling about rubbish on the towpath, a narrowboat approached. I could hear him coming almost before I could see him, his engine was going at full blast and at full screech. A cloud of diesel fumes followed him down the canal. The line of moored boats were rocking and straining at their ropes as he passed. I expected him to slow down as he approached me but he didn't. I ground to a halt and plastered myself against a moored boat hoping he would pass without hitting me. As the boat passed, inches from my portside the angry faced, young, dread-locked man at the helm, screamed down the words of abuse that hadn't yet left my lips.

I was planning on moving down the Thames to Reading and meet up with my sister to travel along the Kennet and Avon. Then she told me she had a bad back and I knew that there are a lot of locks, reportedly heavy, stiff locks, along the Kennet and Avon canal. I changed plans and decided I'd hang around Oxford (if I could find a mooring) and we'd go down the Thames where the locks were manned and she wouldn't have to do any hard work. Once I'd spent time on the Upper Thames, heading to and from Lechlade. I didn't want go head back onto those murky canals anyway. I loved being on the river with deep water under the hull, with bendy curves and wildlife.

Most of the moorings in Oxford are for 48-hours but near Frenchay Bridge there is a seven-day mooring. It was rough and shallow, I definitely needed the gang-plank, and it is away from the city centre (the 48-hour moorings are close to the centre) but it was worth it not to have to keep moving. The walk from the quiet mooring into the centre, touristy part of Oxford was down a street lined with affluent Victorian villas and then into the lively area of Jericho, with its restaurants and cafe, pubs and small shops.

I had visitors when I was in Oxford. For some strange reason when I suggested to friends that they joined me to go from nowhere to nowhere with a lot of locks in between I didn't have any takers. When I said I'm in Oxford for a week but I'm stationary there so, sorry, there won't be any cruising or any locks to work the visitors were queuing up along the towpath.

Oxford is the Oxford seen in travel magazines, on television, in iconic photographs. It is lovely. It is busy. It is touristy. When I was there the students at the university had been replaced with foreign language students which meant just as many bikes but less road sense. I'd lived on the outskirts of Cambridge for many years and I was inclined to compare and contrast Oxford with Cambridge. I was pleased to find they both had an Arts Cinema, and a Loch Fynne restaurant. Cambridge is smaller, more compact. Oxford seems richer. Oxford has more small, individual shops and cafes. Cambridge has better punting.

With all those visitors I regularly toured the sites of Oxford and became familiar with the best walks, the most interesting pubs, the cafes with the most delicious cakes.

I walked the street back to the boat regularly, passed the desirable houses with the well-kept gardens that stretched down to the canal. In the end I got a bit fed-up of foreign students and academics on bikes and the niceness of everywhere and was happy to move down to the 48-hour moorings and wait for my sister to arrive at the nearby railway station.

The Thames

When my sister did arrive she was allowed one day to look around Oxford. It was a whistle-stop tour around the touristy sites and colleges, I'd seen them all before over a number of days, she needed to fit it in to one short day. It was obligatory to go to the Eagle and Child but she was only allowed to down a quick half of cider in there because there were other interesting pubs to visit; pubs that weren't so full of other tourists. Then on to the Bodleian library and a waltz around the Ashmolean. She wasn't allowed to go punting because that was far too leisurely a pastime, we had more colleges to see. In the end we almost jogged around Oxford, but she did get shown all the sights even if they all went past in a blur.

The following morning it was through Isis Lock, make a badly executed turn to go down the Sheepwash Channel, under the pigeon-splattered rail bridge and onto the Thames. We'd done our research before setting off; we'd both read Three Men in a Boat. Over one hundred and twenty years since the book was written the humour of Three Men in a Boat has stood the test of time. Unsurprisingly the geography of the Thames and the positioning of the locks is still the same (almost: one lock has gone). Yet it is the feel of the Thames that most memorably remains; the trip boats, the leisure activities, the boaters and swimmers, the crowds at locks and the long, quiet stretches of water. It is still possible to do what the three men (and the dog) did; hire a camping skiff and row along the Thames. Mind you it's easier, although less adventurous, on a narrow-boat that has all mod cons on board.

I think I would be happy to spend the rest of my life pottering up and down the Thames. I loved this thoroughfare to London. I loved its quiet and secluded reaches, its smart and charming riverside towns. I loved the variety of boats, the historical places, the expensive houses with immaculate lawns falling down to the water, the old manor houses sitting on hills overlooking the river. The locks are manned, well-kept and colourful. To me the Thames has everything a boater could wish for. The only downside is the cost. I don't own one of those houses with the boathouse sheltering the gleaming white cruiser because I can't afford it. Likewise, I wouldn't be able to afford a mooring in the Thames marinas. I'm not sure I can even afford the nightly stopping fees. On the lower Thames, where the few EA moorings are full early in the day (I never got the hang of setting off early and stopping early), the alternative is to pay for nightly, visitor moorings. I never really objected to these because they were in great places that I was lucky to be visiting but I had been lulled into a sense of financial ease with the free moorings of the canal system and didn't factor in this additional cost.

It was only two women, not three men and a dog, in the boat setting off down the Thames on that warm, late July morning. One a supposedly experienced boater, one a comparative novice although when we entered a lock it was difficult to discern with the naked eye which was the experienced boater and which was the novice.

In a Thames lock, a narrowboat should be tethered to the bollards with ropes from the bow and stern. Competent boaters glide into the lock, lasso the bollards, switch off the engine and wait for the lock-keeper to give any instructions to the boater. When going upstream some of the locks are deep and lassoing the bollards is difficult, then the lock keepers lean over with a hook to take the rope and help the boats tie-up. Going downstream should be easier, after all the bollards are mostly level with the feet of the helmsman. For us it wasn't. For some reason we always went into the locks flinging ropes about with gay abandon in the general direction of the lock-side and neither of us ever managed to get one wrapped around the bollard at the first attempt. It was then a case of shunt the boat backwards and forwards; line-up with the bollards; try again; miss again. Sometimes I stepped off the boat but the bow always seemed to be drifting away as I tried to secure the stern rope. It was always heading into the centre of the lock, about to demolish a cruiser or a canoe, and I had to hurriedly hop back on to steer it to safety. If Marcelle got off she invariably tripped over one of bollards instead of looping the rope around it. Then if we were securely tied up it was always in the wrong place and we had to untie to move the boat along. We cruised the Thames together as far as

Windsor and never improved. Lock-keepers laughed and helped us, or tutted and helped us, or were so disgusted with our feeble attempts at throwing the ropes in the general direction of a bollard that they just left us to it and then watched our boat rattle around as the water gushed out of the lock. Each time we entered a lock we said 'we'll do it properly this time,' but we never did.

'What happens if we lose power?' Marcelle asked as we moored opposite the large weir near Abingdon Lock. 'We get dragged over the weir and die,' I told her. At this point I suddenly thought of safety, we were not on a shallow canal, we were on a large river which could be quite ferocious. Admittedly, at the time, it was benign but even so the weirs are fierce and the locks are deep and powerful. I do wear a life-jacket if I'm single-handed on a river, sometimes even on the canals and the sensible thing would be to wear one on the Thames. If I fell in Marcelle would be too absorbed in her book to hear the splash. We donned life-jackets. We never fell in so they weren't needed for saving our lives but they did manage to hamper our rope-throwing activities even more and I kept getting the toggles caught on the Morso handle. I also made sure the anchor was secured to the boat. I gave her instructions, 'If we lose power dash to the bow and throw the anchor over.'

'What will you do?' she asked.

'I shall remain at the stern and panic.'

Off we went on our merry way, after a downpour on our first afternoon the weather improved. The sun shone, the breeze was light, the birds sang. We stopped at Abingdon for the evening and then the following morning had a long, enjoyable, walk around the town. At Shillingford my map suggested there were moorings and we thought to stop there, but most of the nooks and crannies in between the trees already had boats moored in them or were too short for a sixty-footer. Then we saw a reasonable sized space. A small group of teenagers, gathered on the river bank, grinned at us as I stepped onto the uneven bank, rope and mooring pin in hand. I placed the pin in the bank, smacked it with the mallet and a swarm of wasps flew into the air. The teenagers fled in one direction, I fled in the other, Marcelle holding onto the bow rope couldn't see what the fuss was about. Then the swarm headed towards her, she let go of the rope and jumped on board, rapidly closing doors behind her. When I felt it was safe to go outside again we left. The boat had already drifted away from the bank. Not much further we found another, less deadly space. When I walked back along the footpath I found the sign that the teenagers had removed and discarded. It said 'WASPS NESTS! DO NOT MOOR HERE.'

We stopped at Wallingford on their town moorings, where I was shouted at by an elderly man on a smart cruiser for a) inconsiderate mooring and b) being a narrowboat owner ('Narrowboats shouldn't be on this stretch of water,' he screeched). Mooring and leaving gaps between boats so that no one else has room to pull in irritates me and I am careful not to do it myself. In this case I wasn't at fault. The pontoon was empty when I arrived, except for two small boats which I pulled up between, leaving no gaps. Evidently they'd left and the other boats that had tied up since had left unhelpful spaces. If the cruiser owner had spoken politely I'd have been more than happy to pull back but as he was abusive I just suggested a few places where he could put his boat and returned to my lunch. The other main surprise in the attractive town of Wallingford was the signpost that said Oxford 12 miles. We seemed to have been going for days but we were still only 12 miles from Oxford. This river must meander a lot.

We moored the following night at Childs Beale. It is a nature reserve and there is a park and gardens, which were closed so we could only wander around and peer through fences at strange animals. It's a peaceful setting: no noise, no wasps, no teenagers, no irate cruiser owners. Back on the boat we sat quietly in the bow reading, sipping wine, until the light faded. Across the river, a man rowed a small craft. His boat was barely visible against the darkening trees on the far bank but the gentle splash of his oars was magnified by the water. From the woods across the river there came the harsh call of a stag.

At Pangbourne we thought we better stop to have a drink at The Swan; the place where the three men in the boat gave up on the journey. My main memory of Pangbourne is not of its old pubs and the Edwardian elegance of the riverside houses but of a very useful launderette and the large, submerged rocks at the end of the mooring against the meadow where I nearly wrecked my prop.

We went gently on our way through picturesque locks packed with flowers, each one a credit to the lock-keepers who cared for them. We shared locks with expensive cruisers where we had to crane our necks to exchange greetings with their incumbents, sitting high above us on plush banquette seats. We shared with large and daunting tour boats, with small cruisers, rowing eights and vintage Thames skiffs. At one lock, a posse of canoes came in behind me. We chatted as the water went down and as I left the lock one hooked a paddle onto my stern fenders and the rest hung onto him. They laughed as eight canoes tailgated me out of the lock. I laughed but the lock-keeper was cross. He said they were idiots and it was dangerous. Actually he was right, they were idiots for getting so near a spinning

propeller. I was also an idiot for finding it amusing.

I was particularly fascinated by this variety of boats on the Thames, especially the classic or historic boats. The old launches, skiffs and rowing boats in immaculate condition; the teak and brass polished to within an inch of their lives or with blue painted hulls you could see your face in. I fell in love with a 35ft, 1930's launch that was for sale at a boatyard along the way. I think I would have swapped Rea for her immediately, even though she would be totally unsuitable for living on in the winter. Poor Rea. But then I've always been a sucker for a pretty face, I've never been the faithful type.

Through the smart towns of Henley and Marlow where we stopped to window shop but couldn't afford to buy. The Henley Regatta had already taken place although the stands and a marquee still stood, indicative of what a large event the regatta is. It was probably a good job we weren't in the vicinity when it was going on. I hate to think what damage a badly driven narrowboat could cause to fragile rowing boats. We were also told, frequently, we'd just missed the swan upping. This is the traditional and picturesque ritual of a census of the swans on the river. Men (I don't think there are any women swan uppers) in rowing skiffs, wearing bright blazers go around annoying the swans. I would like to have seen that, maybe next time I'll plan my journey better.

We stopped at Cookham because we wanted to visit the Stanley Spencer gallery. I've always loved his pictures of slightly strange shaped people and was looking forward to seeing the originals. They weren't there. His better known paintings were on loan to Compton Verney (I managed to visit them later when I took a bus and a long walk from Banbury). What were there were his huge paintings of the ship works on the Clyde. These were commissioned during the second world war and in their complexity and execution they were stunning and I was more than happy to get the chance to see them.

We stayed in Cookham for a couple of days and visitors arrived for lunch, the intention was to go downriver to Cliveden but it was hot, the wine was cold and we were too lethargic. We just sat in the bow and watched the boaters, walkers and the swimmers: a constantly moving tableau outside the boat and we didn't have to do anything but eat, drink and watch.

The area around Cliveden is beautiful with its high wooded hills and the islands and inlets along the water, but by the following morning we were on a mission to get to Windsor for Marcelle to catch trains and planes and hadn't got time to loiter in scenic and interesting spots. The conurbation of Maidenhead encroached onto the river. Grand houses, expensive hotels, Michelin starred restaurants lined the water's edge; a road ran alongside 48-hour moorings. On the water: trip boats and sculls, cruisers and hire boats. Everything busy, busy in a most picturesque way. Then once under the M4 bridge it all went quiet and rural again. I moored just outside of Windsor and we walked in. It was a longer walk than I had anticipated and I was harangued for mooring there and expecting Marcelle to carry a bag that far. It was dark when we returned, after a Thai meal in the town, we stumbled amongst tree roots and overhanging branches and stopped to listen to owls hooting in the trees. You'd think I'd lived on a boat long enough to know to take a torch with me when I went out in the evening. The following morning, I moved off early and moored in Windsor, an easy suitcase drag to the station, the only downside being that I had to pay for that mooring; the other rougher more distant one had been free.

I did my bit as a tourist in Windsor and Eton before moving on to be a tourist in Runnymede, a place that seemed of more significance to the Americans than to the British. The Magna Carta was signed here. It's the basis of the American Bill of Rights and Constitution and they revere it; to us it's just another bit of history.

I made it as far as a mooring outside the unappetisingly named Slug and Lettuce in Staines. From Staines I had intended to travel down to Brentford and enter the canal system again, moving on up the Grand Union, a section I hadn't travelled on before. I didn't do that. The reason I gave myself was that there was an imminent arrival of a grandchild in Cambridge and it was easier to get to Cambridge from Oxford than some of the places along the Grand Union. This reason was, of course, a load of rubbish, the real reason was I didn't want to relinquish my time on the Thames just yet. I picked up a new crew member at Staines told him he wasn't going where he expected to go and turned back.

The news that my first grandchild had been born came when I was just below Abingdon. I set off for Oxford as dawn cracked. I wished I'd done it more often, this getting up early before the sun had even fully risen. The morning was still and chilly and the sun was just starting to break through the thin clouds on the horizon. Mist floated on the water, ethereal swans gliding in its silver film. Inhabitants of the towns and the boats moored along the river were still in their beds. The water was calm and quiet. The locks were ghost locks, unmanned and empty of all other boats and people. It was so incredibly peaceful. This didn't last long; by the time we reached the outskirts of Oxford the world was waking up, people were about, the traffic noise impinged on the burble of the river. Other boats were starting to move. The river no longer belonged to just me and Rea. As the day came to life, once again, it was everybody's river.

I got to Cambridge later that day and met a small, perfect little boy: my first grandchild.

Part Two – Heading Back

Dreary

The weather report on my phone says the weather today is dreary and it is going to be dreary all day. I think the phone has understated the weather. If I'd been cruising the Llangollen canal along its dramatic viaduct with views across glorious countryside I still think today could be classed as dreary. As I'm on the Grand Union Canal heading towards Birmingham I think the combination of drab weather and buildings that are industrial or derelict, or both, would better be described as totally and utterly depressing.

The boat is sharing the canal with a dead black and white puppy, Tesco's bags, plastic bottles, empty cider cans and myriads of unidentifiable rubbish. The bottom of the boat scraps on debris hidden under water that looks brown and viscous. I decide I'll be extra careful about not falling in the canal. Falling into water like that would be like falling into a vat of sump oil.

The derelict canal side buildings, once a hive of activity, are broken down and daubed with graffiti. There are subdued splashes of colour from the rosebay willowherb, purple loosestrife and dandelions that straggle amongst the brickwork. Buddleia and bramble bushes have colonised the edges of the disused buildings. The tired flowers of the buddleia are more brown than mauve and the bramble leaves are rust edged and their fruit a small dried black instead of a plump purple. On another day I would have been interested in all the old industrial architecture and how nature is reclaiming it. Even in their state of disrepair and vandalism the intricacies of brickwork and the basic solidity of the buildings remain but on a day of low grey cloud and cold relentless drizzle I just find the journey towards Birmingham uninspiring.

I moor up at Aston, I don't want to go any further because I'm picking up Steve tomorrow and if I have to do eleven locks of the Aston Flight and another thirteen on the Farmers Bridge Flight (if I actually decide to go into Birmingham) then I prefer to have help. Anyway I'm cold and fed-up and even if it is only the beginning of September there is the feeling that autumn and winter are on the way and that thought makes me feel even more depressed.

When I moor up for the night in urban areas I usually choose places where other boats are moored, or under CTV cameras. Here at Aston there is a long stretch of canal with only one boat tied up and it would appear that it doesn't have residents on board. This is not a good sign, if nobody moors along an urban stretch of canal there is usually a good reason for it. I tie up. Across the canal is an office block and underground car park, this would be populated and reassuring on a week day but on a Saturday afternoon it is empty and quiet. On the other side of the hedge is a blank, empty space cleared for future building.

I lock up the boat and walk down the canal to see if I can find a spot that I feel more comfortable with. The buildings of Aston University are along here but term has not yet started and they are locked and empty. There are a few men walking the towpath, alone or in two's or three's all looking slightly down at heel. On a building site there are four men, loading goods into a white van, they stop working and stare at me walking past. I feel they stare malevolently at me, but I may just be getting paranoid. Ahead of me on the towpath three youths are swigging from cans and throwing the empties into the canal so they can try to sink them with stones. My mooring by the side of the office block and empty space suddenly seems to be a haven of calm and tranquillity so I turn and once more walk past the malevolent stares of the white van men and go back to the boat.

Once I am on the boat, securely locked in and have got the curtains closed and the dinner cooking and once I have got half way through the bottle of wine I start to feel a bit easier about the place I am moored and, after all, it is only for one night. I go to bed and sleep fitfully, unusual for me as I normally sleep the sleep of the dead. At odd times throughout the night I hear voices passing by my window only feet from where I try to sleep. At four in the morning somebody goes by singing at the top of their voice. Otherwise, nothing happens. Nobody tries to break into the boat. No drunks think it is good fun to untie the boat or run along the roof or hammer on the windows as they pass by. I stay safe and sound but when morning comes I wake early and I keep a look-out for my travelling companion. I am happy to see him, just after eight am, staggering towards me. He must plan on being on board for a while because he's carrying enough beer and provisions to last the next six months.

Birmingham

It seems it's my turn to do the locks; bad back (probably from carrying all that beer on board) and fragile shoulders are given as a reason for not doing the physical work. I suppose it's true it is my turn to do some serious wheel locking instead of just staring at blank greasy walls as the boat drifts downwards into locks. I actually prefer to work the locks instead of standing at the helm doing very little except showing off my steering skills by threading a six-foot ten-inch boat into little more than seven-foot gap without touching the sides.

The thirteen locks of the Farmers Bridge Flight are hard work, after the first three I'm starting to doubt my premise that I prefer to do the locks and I'm wondering if it is worth all this effort to go down the flight just to spend a few days in Birmingham and then turn around and come back again.

Birmingham has developed around this canal: it was once (in the 1800's and early 1900's) a scene of great industrial activity before it declined into a scene of urban decay. Now a policy of urban regeneration means it is on the up once more. This flight of locks goes from where the Digbeth branch joins at Aston Junction through to the developments around Cambrian Wharf and Brindley Place and onto the old Gas Street Basin. Yet despite all the new building there are still many reminders of the old canal system; the heritage of the canals is snuggled in amongst the new developments. The arched red brick bridges cross the canals and there are the bricked-up archways that used to lead into the branches of the Birmingham Canal Network (BCN) and wharves of the old warehouses. Now they lead to flattened land awaiting new developments or are used as car parks sometimes they appear to arrive at the doors of a new block of offices. Old warehouses are still in evidence; many now converted to offices, some to flats and all are overshadowed by the new high-rise buildings around them. There is a common saying that Birmingham has more canals than Venice, it may have been true in the heyday of the canals but now with many of the branches closed it is unlikely to be so. Of course one shouldn't confuse quantity with quality. These stretches of industrial canals are unlikely to attract coachloads of tourists and they definitely won't have cruise ships visiting so the thousands of passengers can get off to photograph glorious, medieval palaces. Yet although they cannot compete with the magnificence of Venice these locks, redundant wharves and red brick warehouses and bridges are interesting and they do have a beauty of their own.

When the buildings become more distant from the edges of canal and towpath, the Post Office Tower looms ahead and a new bridge, decorative with white arches frames new blocks of flats. Then working down the flight the supports of an office block straddle the canal. Underneath the building the lack of light means the stones and brickwork of the canal sides are moss strewn and mildewed. The road bridge ahead is up a steep flight of steps lined with graffiti. The high brick arches under a railway crossing are of a forbidding blackened brick, and huge wooden doors, securely locked, stand underneath the arches. There is a pile of damp clothes heaped against the lock side; t-shirt, jeans, underpants and socks. I wonder if they were left behind from a brief Saturday night sexual encounter, a drunken push into the water or a suicide attempt. I fill the lock half expecting the turbulence of the water to bring a body to the surface but only a few beer cans and take-away cartons flurry back and forth in the eddies of the black water. Perched on the arches of the underground car-park a heron watches us; he is still and serious until a child on the towpath shouts and the echo reverberates around the concrete supports. He takes flight slowly and gracefully spreading his wide wings and flying back low over the flight of locks into an open sky.

At the bottom of the flight, to the left, there are boats moored in Cambrian Wharf. It would appear that now the locks are behind us and there's water-borne traffic ahead of us it's my turn to drive. We pass under three road bridges and into an open space of water with the glass and concrete of the National Indoor Arena (NIA) ahead. There is a roundabout in the middle of the canal. A roundabout isn't a common sight on a canal and I'm unsure about the protocol for negotiating waterway roundabouts. Is it the same as a road or different?

On roads we drive on the left, on the canals we drive on the right. Which way should I go around a canal roundabout? On the roundabout is a fingerpost with directions and mileage down the four alternate routes. I'm hesitating, I'm too far away too read the signs and I can see boats approaching from two of the other directions. I wait to see which of the boats has priority. I think it must be the green, narrowboat approaching from the left and turning right rather than the trip boat approaching from the right and going straight ahead. The green boat thinks he has priority as well and starts his turn, the trip boat steams on ahead missing the green boat's bow by inches causing him to engage reverse thrust quickly, panic and hit the island. Obviously on a Birmingham canal the rules of the road don't apply; trip boats always have priority. It's fair enough I suppose, they are bigger, faster and they do have to earn their keep, waiting around while some elderly, leisure boater dithers at the junction will cost them money. I do think that, on a busy day, this junction could be an interesting place to be a spectator.

Slowly into Birmingham, jazz is blasting out from the Malt House pub, there is a queue outside the Sea Life Centre which stands to our right then it's into Brindley Place with its bars and restaurants. The smell of burgers makes me feel hungry. The café boat is full and there is a queue for the trip boat. The bridge from Brindley Place over to the Symphony Hall is busy and a banner hanging from the bridge advertises a charity Dragon Boat Race in a few weeks' time. Through the tunnel under Broad Street and into Gas Street Basin with its moored boats to the left and a narrow stretch which used to be a stop lock. There are no longer gates here, the need to protect the loss of precious water to rival canal companies (from Birmingham Canal Navigations to Worcester and Birmingham Canal) but the seven-foot stretch of concrete remains. There's an audience sitting at the tables squeezed outside a café but unusually for me, when faced with an audience, I steer properly and I glide through without touching the sides. Ahead of us a boat is leaving so I wait until he has moved away and moor up in his vacated spot in front of a converted warehouse which advertises itself as a club but seems to be empty and unused. Maybe, at 3am tomorrow morning when the repetitive beat is reverberating around the boat I will find out I am mistaken and wish I'd stayed on my quiet, if slightly creepy, mooring at Aston. I'm in Birmingham. Was the hard work of coming down (and going back up) all those locks worth it? No doubt I'll find out in the next few days.

The mooring in Gas Street Basin was certainly busier than the previous night but I slept soundly and peaceably, here in Central Birmingham I don't feel the unease I'd felt the previous night. I'm not sure it would have been quite as peaceful if I'd been here on a Saturday night instead of the Sunday. I was only a stone's throw from Broad Street with all its bars, restaurants and clubs. Broad Street on a Friday or Saturday night is a sight to behold especially when the hen and stag night parties are out in force. There are an amazing number of small, leather nurse's outfits stretched over large amounts of flesh (the bride-to-be is always identifiable because she wears a short veil). Perfume and after-shave hang in the air mixing with the aromas of chips, onions, burgers and curry. The parties of leather clad nurses get more raucous as the night goes on; the more subdued stag parties shrink in to the dark corners of the bars as they hear the hen parties approaching.

I find one of the best parts of being on a boat is the change of location, one day in a quiet rural setting, another moored outside a boater's pub, sometimes moored outside small country towns with farmers' markets and expensive dress shops and charity shops that are stocked with designer dresses (none of which ever fit me). Now I have my own apartment in the centre of Birmingham. I walk around and admire the impressive, Roman-style, early 19th century town hall with the steps leading down to a large fountain with a large lady wallowing in it (I'm told it's locally known as the Floozie in the Jacuzzi). The gardens surrounding 18th century Birmingham Cathedral are attractive. The Jewellery Centre and the St Paul's area, where the older buildings remain as a beacon to Victorian building, still hold the resonance of the craftsmen and women who worked here not so very long ago. The uniform local red brick, with little visible mortar showing, is both stately and solid and the intricacies of the darker brick add interest around windows and under eaves. I believe a lot of this substantial industrial architecture has been lost in the 20th Century, some to the Luftwaffe but more to the city planners. There is now a better appreciation of all things industrial (including the canal system) and hopefully what is left will be preserved and not demolished although I won't hold my breath on that one.

I make the most of my week in Birmingham. I'd hoped to view the Staffordshire hoard which was found a couple of years previously but only a few items are on display as the gallery for their use has yet to be completed. I visited the museums and galleries, having tea in the Art Gallery café where murals overlook the customers, and where finding a table clear of used crockery and clutter is a challenge. The library is still a work in progress. The yellow hoops of its façade overlook Centenary Square and the circular Hall of Memory.

I go to the Electric Cinema and sit in comfortable chairs sipping wine while I watch the film. I sit in pubs and listen to music and to the local accents. The Birmingham accent has many detractors and along with the Liverpool accent has regularly been voted the worst in Britain but I could listen to it for hours. It is another thing I enjoy about moving round the country: listening to the variation in local accents. Even though I have been trying for years to rid myself of my Hull accent (unsuccessfully, I may add) I hope other people hang onto their local accent.

I'm not a shopper, the thought of entering a modern shopping centre gives me a similar feeling to being asked to walk through a snake pit so I manage to avoid visiting the shops of the Bullring. I walk through them and down steep steps to go to Birmingham's splendid food market. Birmingham is definitely a hilly city, as all these steps and as all those locks leading up or down into the city will testify. I may dislike shops but I love markets, especially markets like this one. It is this place that really shows the cultural diversity of Birmingham; the okra, yams, plantains, bunches of green bananas, mangoes, pineapples, star fruit and lychees share space with the more mundane carrots and potatoes. Some fruit and vegetables, I don't recognise. I keep asking other shoppers what's that, how do you cook this? In the meat market a row of pigs' heads sits neatly above their severed trotters. Chinese women barter over an ugly fish with a big head, a fish that is unknown to me. I buy lots of fruit and vegetables because it is so cheap and so fresh then after the toil back to the boat with arms stretched a few extra inches I realise it will take me a month to eat it all so most will end up being thrown away. No handy freezers on my boat, they use too much electricity. I go into the Sexy Shop next to the market. Their goods are sensible night dresses and big knickers, underwear that would pass as sexy only to an octogenarian having trouble with his cataracts. The knickers I buy are substantial and only cost a pound each but I find another bag to put them in; I don't want to walk through Birmingham with a bag that has 'Sexy Shop' written all over it.

James Brindley, the father of the canal system, is in evidence here in Birmingham. There is Brindley Place and the James Brindley Pub. It was the brilliance of the pioneering engineers of the 1700's that made the canals a lasting and viable proposition. James Brindley, in particular, was at the forefront of developing the Grand Cross that carried goods from mines, quarries and factories throughout the Midlands.

So was the trail of thirteen locks into the city worth it? Yes. To be in the centre of a vibrant city livened me up and will make me appreciate the contrast of quiet countryside when I reach it. Whether I will still think that all the locks were worth it when I am halfway back up the flight is debateable. It appears it is still my turn to do the lock wheeling.

Captain Splendid

I put the boat into the fourth lock on the Aston flight and the gate won't fully close. I poke behind the gates with the boat hook, sweep the boat pole in the deeper water around the centre but don't dislodge anything. Steve joins me and we fiddle about a bit trying out various options. I even try to fill the lock without the gate being fully closed, needless to say that doesn't work it just starts to drain the entire canal system. A woman from the boat following me comes along to see what the delay is and we all go through the same procedure of trying to clear the obstruction with the same result: the gate won't close. I move my boat out of the lock to give us more room to poke about; poke about a bit more and still the lock gate won't fully close. We make the joint decision to call C&RT. They're not far away in the centre of Birmingham and it will give them something to do on this quiet and fine Sunday morning.

But fear not faint-hearted boaters: help is on the way! In the distance and approaching at speed is our knight, not in shining armour but a tatty t-shirt, not on a noble stallion but on a battered old bike but the effect is the same or well … a bit similar. He's hunched over the handle-bars, knobbly knees working like pistons, grey hair streaming in the wind and under his arm he is carrying a boat pole as if it is a jousting spear. It's Captain Splendid! The only thing missing is some accompanying music such as The Ride of the Valkeries.

I had rung C&RT and was settling back for an interesting conversation about the performance of Michael MacIntyre who the crew of the following boat had been to see the previous evening in Birmingham. Because I live a TV-free existence I have never heard of Michael MacIntyre and was unsure whether he was a singer, comedian or juggler. She is saying how funny he was (hah, he must be a comedian) when Captain Splendid skids to a halt next to us. He has no time for small talk or talk of any kind for that matter, he hardly makes any eye contact as we tell him the gate won't close. He has a mission to accomplish! He has an itinerary to stick to! He can't waste time because of jammed lock gates! He ignores us totally and vigorously pokes around near the lock entrance and locates a solid obstruction. He pushes at it and when that fails to dislodge it he swears at it a few times (a device I often use to remove jammed objects and I can tell him, from experience, it doesn't work).

He mutters to no-one in particular that he needs more equipment to dislodge the obstruction: jumps back on his bike, wobbles a bit as he puts his barge pole back under his arm wobbles a bit more and then pedals away furiously down the towpath to get more appropriate object removing equipment.

My new found friend from the following boat and I raise our eyebrows at each other, shrug our shoulders and lean on the open lock gate so as to continue the conversation about Michael MacIntyre. We both stumble backwards as the gate closes.

So I call C&RT back to tell them we have been rescued by a passing knight in dinghy armour, put my boat back in the lock, fill it up and go on my way before Captain Splendid can return with his full complement of equipment for removing obstacles from behind lock gates.

Alrewas

At Alrewas the canal joins the Trent River for the short journey between Alrewas Lock and Wychnor Lock. The heavy rain has caused the waters of the Trent to rise and the lock is closed. I manage to get a mooring slot close to the closed lock and sit it out to wait for the rain to cease and the lock to re-open. It is not a great hardship for Alrewas is a pleasant place to spend a few days. I walk back along the towpath to Fradley Junction to meet up with friends in the Black Swan, a pub allegedly devoted to boaters, which today is full of leather-clad bikers drinking coke and orange juice. My friends are turning left at the junction to travel along the west bound Trent and Mersey and eventually to travel to Llangollen. I spend the following evening in a pub at Alrewas watching a game of Aunt Sally. It seems a vicious game, the club is thrown over-arm at the hapless image of Aunt Sally but I never do work out how the game is scored and how the winner is decided. I had seen the game played when I was in Oxford. It is good to see these old pub games still being played and to see the regional variations. In Northamptonshire it was a game of skittles played with heavy flat wooden discs; in Oxfordshire it's Aunt Sally; in Birmingham some of the pubs have crown green bowling greens attached to their gardens. I'll just have to spend more time travelling and visiting pubs to investigate other regional variations.

I walk past the closed lock to look at the state of the river. It is definitely in spate: the water flows from the left just beyond the lock gates and with great force bends around to become the navigable part of the Trent. The rest of the water crashes over a large unprotected weir. Looking at the amount of water passing down and over that weir I'm glad not to be travelling on it. I can see the point of closing the lock and I can't imagine that volume of water will subside for at least a week to allow boats passage for the few miles of river journey.

Three days later the lock is opened and I'm the second boat in the queue. That morning rumours had travelled along the line of waiting boats that the lock would be opened in the afternoon and I had gone for a walk to see the state of the river. To me it still looked ferocious and long sweep of the unprotected weir where the river met the canal still looked threatening.

I waited my turn to pass through the lock feeling a sense of trepidation. I was nervous about that weir and, as I was travelling downstream with the heavy flow of water, I knew I would have less steerage. I planned to stay as near to the left bank as possible to keep away from the pull of the weir. As I would then basically be driving on the wrong side of the canal I hoped I wouldn't meet a boat coming the other way. I left the lock and met a boat coming the other way. I had to move rapidly to the right and towards the weir, I put on more throttle and that, combined with the heavy flow of the river, shot me safely past the weir onto the main, calmer, navigable stretch of water.

The oncoming boat went past in a blur. 'I bet you haven't been white water rafting on a narrowboat before,' shouted the woman on the other boat as I zoomed by her.

Considering I was on a narrowboat I was travelling fast (maybe almost seven miles an hour) and it was glorious. I was back on the move and I was on a river after weeks of canal life and I was happy. I have never been a speed junkie; basically you can keep anything that goes faster than a galloping horse, but the pleasure I got from that short rapid journey to Wychnor Lock did make me think that maybe I'm not cut out for the slow pace of life on the canals and perhaps a narrowboat isn't my ideal mode of transport.

Going Home

Winter looms. My original intention was to winter on the canals but it is getting colder and the nights are darker and a winter moored against a dark towpath where I knew nobody and I would have to move the boat every two weeks, whatever the weather, is losing its appeal. I call the managers of my old mooring at Oundle and the answer is, 'Yes we have a space and you can come back.'

It's the end of October and the clocks had just been put back. When the clocks are changed it always seems they steal an hour of daylight from the entire day not just put the darkness forward an hour. The weather is wet and getting wetter. As I reach the Nene so does the water from its catchment areas to the west and south of Northampton and Strong Stream Advice is issued. On previous occasions I've moored at the town quay in Northampton, an area with a bad reputation amongst boaters but an area where I've always felt perfectly safe. There are always a few homeless drinkers on the riverside benches and drunks singing their way over the bridge in the early hours of the morning. There are always lads messing around on bikes but none of the behaviour has ever seemed threatening. In addition, the number of CCTV cameras trained on the flats and walkways does give me a feeling of security. This time, however, I have to go to London for a few days for work and although I don't mind being on the boat along the quayside in Northampton I am not so happy to leave Rea by herself in the long, dark nights with rising river levels and strong winds forecast.

I book into Northampton Marina for the duration of the Strong Stream Advice and head off to London without having to worry about what is happening to Rea. Three days later when I return from London the sun is shining and the river levels around Northampton have subsided. I feel I could happily venture out from the marina now but because there are still high-water levels and flooding in the lower reaches of the Nene, around Dog in the Doublet Lock, Strong Stream Advice has not been lifted and many of the locks are still reversed. The EA wait until the full length of the Nene is safe to travel on and don't re-open the locks until all fifty miles have cleared.

It would probably be safe to travel the approximately thirty miles to Oundle; the locks along this stretch have been re-opened but if I travel when the advice notice is still in force my insurance policy would be invalid. So again I sit it out, waiting for locks to be re-opened. It's not bad being here, the laundry and the shower block facilities are excellent, there is water and pump-out facilities on site. As an extra bonus I am plugged into an electricity supply. This constant supply of electricity without having to consider how much I am running down the batteries is a great novelty. I can have all the lights on, I can use my computer whenever I want and if it's cold I can just put on the electric fire and not light the stove. I am so enamoured with this constant supply of electricity that I go around the boat not switching lights off behind me, not worrying if I am leaving the computer on and even using my CD player with gay abandon. I'm even tempted to go into Northampton and buy a kettle and a hair-dryer not because I need a kettle or a hair-dryer but just to celebrate the fact that I have enough wattage to run them.

On a Tuesday evening the Strong Stream Advice is lifted and I prepare myself for an early start the next morning to take maximum advantage of the diminishing daylight hours. The night is stormy and a high wind buffets the boat; its sound alternates between howling angrily across the marina or whining miserably through the telegraph wires. I always find high winds exhilarating at first and then the noise starts to become increasingly more disturbing. Horses get skittish on a day of high winds, children in school playgrounds become boisterous and boaters become nervous. I switch the radio on and leave it on throughout the night to block out the noise of the wind and the intermittent pulses of rain hammering on the roof. When I wake the radio is still on and the shipping forecast is warning of gales force 8 or 9 in Rockall and Cromarty. I crawl out of bed; dress, untie the boat and set off in the grey dawn. Turning out of the marina and towards Becket's Park Lock I find the lock is already being set by another early riser and I join up with a two people travelling in a fifty-foot boat along the Nene to a mooring on the Great Ouse. It is the girl's boat, she's just

77

bought it to live on and her ex-boyfriend has come aboard to help her move it. The reality of driving it has so traumatised her that she has locked herself into the bedroom and doesn't want to come out so effectively we are two boats travelling single-handed for the first few locks. Four hours later at Whiston Lock she eventually ventures out to help work the lock. Three locks further on at Doddington she had been persuaded to try steering the boat. She brought it into the lock nervously but perfectly and from then on either steered the boat or operated the lock with a smile on her face.

Thankfully the weather this morning is a little calmer than the previous night. It's mild for the beginning of November but it's a blustery day; clouds of varying tones of grey are scudding across the sky, shafts of sunlight suddenly shine through blue gaps in the cloud and then just as suddenly both the blue and the sunlight are gone. Rooks wheel and dive high above the boat, black shapes constantly moving against the paler greys of the sky then almost disappearing from view when they are against the black clouds. It would be a great day for an exhilarating walk in the hills but it's not a great day for taking a sixty-foot narrowboat along the twisty River Nene. I wouldn't normally choose to travel on a day like today but more heavy rain is forecast and if I don't leave now I risk being stranded here for the rest of the winter.

Although it is windy, it is mainly a back wind that doesn't cause too much trouble. I don't find moving in this strong wind much of a problem (it's the tying up when single-handed that I find a problem). I put enough revs to counter-balance the wind and although I may appear to be travelling

78

along like a crab, progress is good and uneventful; uneventful that is until I come across a herd of canoeists. It's November for God's sake. What are six novice canoeists doing out on the river? Normally I would slow down and gradually ease my way through them but when I start to slow the wind wants to push me into the reeds. In addition, the canoeists aren't very competent and the sight of a large lump of steel bearing down on them sends panic waves through the group; paddles flail in all directions and one canoe shoots off under my bows. Luckily it lodges itself in the reed bed not under me. When I've managed to avoid that canoe the wind has plastered the other five canoes against the side of my boat. I shout to them that I have to put on acceleration to avoid squashing their companion and I move along the river at a fair pace with the canoes bumping along my side until, one by one, they peel off and then paddle frantically to avoid being shredded by my propeller. Once they've escaped from the side of my boat they look so relieved that I haven't the heart to tell them that behind me, still hidden by the bend, there is another narrowboat.

Despite unexpected canoeists and all the twists and turns of the river there is only a side wind at one lock which pushes both our boats into the weedy bank on the other side of the river instead of against the lock landing. It takes an age to extricate ourselves but eventually we do and get through the lock. It is an advantage that when travelling downriver we don't have to tie-up after the lock to close the guillotine gates. When the gates are open we can just steam off out of the lock giving enough acceleration to counteract the strength of the wind.

There are seventeen locks between Northampton Town and the moorings at Irthlingborough which we hope to reach before dark. It's a lot of locks but the advantage of having to negotiate them on a cold day is that moving about winding paddles and tying up boats does give a much needed chance to get the circulation moving and to make hot coffee. I may have called the day mild but I soon become chilled standing on the back of the boat. Inside the boat is lovely and warm, I put my cast-iron casserole on top of the stove and a stew simmers away happily, every so often sending delicious whiffs through the cabin to my place at the tiller. I just hope I don't have any dramatic crashes and catapult my supper off the top of the stove and all over the floor. I stoke the fire regularly, at first with the pieces of wood that I'd collected on the way, but the wood is a bit damp and although once it gets fully alight it gives off more heat than coal, when it is first put on the fire it produces a lot of smoke. I stand at the back of the boat getting a face full of smoke. There is an old film with Ingrid Bergman where she stands at the bow of a ship with the wind streaming in her face and her hair blowing behind her, on the masts of the ship the flags blow in the opposite direction. I feel there is a similar phenomenon on my boat; the wind is behind us but the smoke blows in my face and although, because the strong flow of the river is with me, I am moving faster than usual on a narrowboat I am hardly moving fast enough to create my own slipstream. I put more logs on the fire when we are in the lock and the smoke trapped between the lock walls nearly asphyxiates the crew of both boats, after that I stick to using coal; it's not free heat like the wood or as hot but it doesn't smoke.

We reach the moorings at Irlingborough, next to the Rushden and Diamonds football ground, as the winter darkness becomes all enveloping. This long stretch of mooring was built by Doc Martens to encourage boaters to moor up and visit their factory outlet. Now that Doc Martens have moved and the Rusden and Diamonds club are in decline so are the moorings. They used to have pump-out and water points now they have neither and the sides of the wooden pontoons are deteriorating but it's dark now and I'm tired so who cares that the moorings are becoming derelict.

The next morning, before dawn, I hear my travelling companion's boat cough into life and they set off leaving me to travel on by myself. I don't know what I did to upset them; we seemed to be getting on fine.

By the time I get myself organised the morning sun is out and the wind has abated. It's become easy boating and as long as the strong pull from some of the weirs is avoided the well maintained and automated locks are easy for me to manage alone. At Lower Ringstead Lock I meet up with another boat, a proper old live-aboard weighed down by a roof full of wood and manned by a taciturn older man and the obligatory large, hairy dog. I wish I'd met up with him one lock earlier then we could at least have shared the hard work of winding the manual wheel at Upper Ringstead. Neither he nor his dog are very friendly, although after working three locks together we are getting into the usual 'boaters travelling

81

though locks together' conversation of 'where are you heading?', 'weather a bit better today', 'there's a mooring (water, pub, facilities, diesel, shop) just after the next lock'. I do get the feeling that if he thought I knew anything at all about engines and gear boxes he would be willing to enter into long conversations but when he asks me what engine I have and I have to think before I answer he, quite rightly, writes me off as a mechanical ignoramus. Yet whatever he lacks in small talk he is efficient when working through the locks so, once I have upped my game to match his efficiency, we make good progress.

By the time we reach Titchmarsh Lock the afternoon sun is dipping low; a red ball over Aldwinckle Lake. I am cold and stumble stiffly off the boat skidding on the wet pontoon. As we had progressed down the Nene the locks became further apart and standing still on the back of the boat was becoming a chilly experience. There were no more wheels to get the circulation moving, no chance to get some hot spicy soup into me when the chill was starting to penetrate the bones. The guillotine gates aren't much help either after the initial burst of energy required to tie up the boats and wind up the paddles on the upper gates the lower guillotine gates just require a three-minute lean on the button as they slowly clank open or shut. There is no hurrying a guillotine gate. I just had to stand and get colder, trying to jump up and down only meant my finger slipped off the button and I got puzzled frowns from my travelling companion who was wondering why the gate kept stopping. I thought of Bob, a regular Nene boater, who has home-made handles to help with the wheels and a contraption of elastic and corks to hold down the buttons. I, of course, had pooh-paahed these prototypes saying they were quite unnecessary. I wished I had one now, then I could have warmed up by doing star jumps along the lock-side while one of these devices kept the button depressed.

I was thinking of stopping at Titchmarsh, there were still two more locks and about an hour and a half of increasingly cold travelling in failing light before I reached my destination. I shiveringly stood with my thumb on the button and watched the dripping gate gradually open. Two red kites circled overhead in a leisurely manner calling to each other. These large birds, with their distinctive forked tails steering them around the skies, with the sound of their Fi Fi Fi call are the sight and the sound that I associate with last winter's mooring near Oundle. Their presence showed I was nearing my destination.

Although the temptation to stop for the night was strong I didn't really have far to go. Even if I arrived in the dark at least I would be home and if I wished I could stay in bed, comfortable and warm, for all of the following day or even for the following four months if I so fancied.

Part Three – Then Came the Rain

The Floods

In January I went to Italy, supposedly to look after my sister when she was discharged from hospital after an operation. While I was there I had a fall on the ice and had an allergic reaction to the ibuprofen I took to ease the pain of my bruised back. I then had an upset stomach and was confined to bed so when she was released from hospital she had to look after me instead of me looking after her.

I left Italy in mid-February. During my stay, the temperature in the Italian mountains had never been above freezing and the snow fall had been heavy. On the last morning in Italy, when I stood on the station platform in Sondrio waiting for a late arriving train, the temperature was $-14°$. In Milan the temperature was still $-9°$ and when I was sitting in a chilly bar drinking a lukewarm coffee that never reached my numb bones I thought I would never be warm again.

Arriving back in Oundle the temperatures of just above freezing seemed balmy in comparison to those of the Italian mountains. The dusk was gathering as I trundled my case through the farm gate that led down to the moorings. In the humpy field lumpy, grey sheep merged with the grey remnants of snow. The hum of generators drifted up from the river bank. I picked my way through the mud and pot holes on the steep track down towards the river. The residue of the sunset was reflecting dark shades of pink and red on the river, the scent of wood smoke was in the air and patches of pale, yellow light from the windows of the boats glimmered on the wet, grassy bank. When I reached Rea I could see the glow of the fire through the window. I had phoned Bill to tell him I was on my way home and he had lit my fire and run the engine to make sure my batteries were charged. When I stepped aboard an all-enveloping warmth greeted me. I closed the curtains, lit the candles heated the spicy chicken bento I'd picked from Wasabi on Kings Cross Station and opened the wine. I put on Radio Four, wrapped the throw around my legs, ate the food. With a glass of wine in hand I settled down cosily with my book for my first evening on board for a month, happy to be back on Rea and once more in love with my boat.

Having to catch up on the work I'd missed when I'd been away I spent a week in London. London doesn't have weather or maybe it's just that the awareness of weather is mitigated by the buildings and traffic. I was only aware it was raining a lot because I arrived at my jobs with sodden hair and clothing but once safely ensconced in offices and underground trains I didn't register just how much rain was falling. I found out when I went back to the boat. The road from the farm gate to my mooring is rough and potted at the best of times and after weeks of heavy rain this was not the best of times. I bumped my way down the track trying to drive around the deep, water filled gullies and parked next to my boat. The river was rushing past relentlessly; a turgid brown flow carrying a myriad of debris with it. Yet in times of flooding a boat is not a bad place to be. It has one major advantage over a house: it floats. When the river is rising and house-owners are putting the sand bags at the door and taking valuables upstairs all a boat dweller has to do is to check that the boat is securely fastened with enough play in the ropes to allow it to rise without being pulled over and then they sit back and wait. The other advantage of a boat is that it is largely self-sufficient; there is no reliance on the national grid for heating and lighting. The electricity is supplied by solar panels or by running the engine or by a generator, the gas comes in bottles, the stove is fired by wood and coal. I can listen to the news and feel sorry for the people who have had to move out of flooded homes but at the same time feel smug that I am warm, cosy and dry and have all facilities on board.

The natural habitat for a boat is water so for boaters water is a good thing but then we can get too much of a good thing. I started to feel less smug when another few days of constant rain caused the river to rise even further and I woke up to find that I couldn't get off the boat. My walk-way was completely under water. The milk-crate that I had been using to step on and off, once the boat had risen high above the pontoon, had been washed away and I was left stranded on board. The cavalry, in the form of the Mechanical Magician and Alan, arrived later in the morning with a combination of platforms, rails and scaffold poles to make a Heath Robinson structure to cross the flooded bank and reach a concrete platform at the stern of my boat. They borrowed a boy to do the nasty cold bit of securing bolts underwater. Even after they'd cobbled together their structure the original concrete platform was too far under water for me to be able to reach it and they had to add concrete breeze blocks so that I could step down onto them.

Yet even those extra breeze blocks weren't enough as the rain continued to fall and the river continued to rise. The breeze blocks disappeared under water. As long as I was wearing wellies I could stand on the gunwales and waggle my leg around until my foot located the breeze block and I could stand on it. Then I would step down into the deeper water that covered the platform and paddle to the shore. Carrying shopping back to the boat wasn't easy and coming home late from the clubhouse after a few glasses of wine was positively precarious.

Yet More Water

In March just when we thought it was safe to go back on the water the gods of inclement weather once again railed against us. There were two days of constant heavy rain, the river rose and for the third time that winter the water was racing past the boat and I had to paddle through floodwater to reach the bank. The Environment Agency again issued Strong Stream Advice, reversed the locks and stood back to see what happened. They admitted that with the Washes in the Northampton area full all the water meadows flooded and with all locks, sluice gates and weirs fully opened, to enable as much water as possible to pass down the river to the sea, there was little else they could but stand and wait. Even the ducks had decamped to the marinas and in-filled gravel pits; they had more sense than to venture out onto that rushing river. Boats were all, hopefully, tied up tightly but with enough slack to rise with the river.

My boat was once again high above the mooring although I could just get out at the bow if I suspended myself on the gunwale and lowered myself gently onto the walkway. I have inherited my father's short legs and I often curse him for it. When I was younger it was the aesthetics of having short legs that concerned me, when I am trying to get on and off a boat it is the practicality of short legs that are the problem. I also had to remember which leg has the dodgy knee and hip. If I get it wrong I'm suspended with one leg out of the boat on the pontoon and one inside but too stiff to lift over the gunwale. I can be stuck like that for a long time. There is always the possibility that when I arrived home late at night the river would have risen a little more and I wouldn't be able to get on the bow of the boat at all and would have to paddle out to the make-shift structure at the stern which had deteriorated into a very wobbly contraption. The front walkway had a dip half way along and that was always under water so I had to paddle through that and as my left wellie had sprung a leak I had one permanently wet foot.

I wasn't planning on going anywhere but there is a psychological difference between not planning on going anywhere and not being able to go anywhere so all this rain and all this water and once again Strong Stream Advice being issued was irritating me. My herbs, which I had moved back to their rightful place under the trees, were now completely submerged and I couldn't be bothered to wade out to rescue them yet again. It was a bit premature of me to remove them from the dryer place higher up near the path but passing dogs kept peeing on them. Maybe that was what gave my casseroles their distinctive taste.

On a more positive note the Met Office wasn't forecasting much rain for this area in the following few days. Looking at my well-worn, favourite site the EA River and Sea Levels the levels at the gauging stations upstream were slowly going down, the standing water was draining away from the fields opposite and sheep had re-appeared at the top end of one field. There was only one flood alert and that was at Cogenhoe Caravan Site but that was okay as Cogenhoe Caravan Site always seems to be underwater and it does make one wonder why they built it there in the first place.

The other thing I noticed was the flow in my water feature. Last December when the flooding was at its worst a spring bubbled up (actually there were three springs bubbling) in the bank across the roadway. With a little help from men with spades I channelled them across the roadway and down the middle of my mooring where a soak-away had previously been constructed. It became quite an impressive steam, we thought of naming it and putting a notice 'Beware of The Ford' in front of it. It ran so clear we even thought of bottling it and selling it as our own mineral water (as Hills and Hollows Essence of Sheep because the sheep field is above it). The birds loved it when all else was frozen they had a fresh source of water, even the ducks came out of acres of river to paddle in it (ducks do that, leave a river full of water to paddle in puddles a few inches deep, I've never worked out why; maybe they just get fed-up of swimming). I could lie in bed at night and listen to the sound of a waterfall. I was even planning on buying a fishing gnome to stand by its side and fish. Then it started to dry up and the rain during the week didn't make it flow faster, so maybe out there the land wasn't as soggy as it was a couple of months ago. Maybe the river would go down quickly and maybe, at the very least, I'd be able to take the boat down to the King's Head at Wadenhoe and maybe spring would arrive and be followed by a glorious summer. Maybe I'd be able to go off and cruise the canal system as I was planning to do. Maybe

On the Move - Briefly

Strong Stream Advice was lifted in April. At the end of April my sister came over from Italy and met up with me in Oundle and her friend Chris joined us. My intention was to get to Peterborough then we'd go back to Oundle to collect cars, Chris would take Marcelle to the airport. I'd go to London for a couple of days' work then I'd re-join the boat and head across to The Great Ouse for four weeks. I'd visit family and catch up with friends in the Cambridge area, after that I'd return the way I'd come and head over to the canal system and probably over-winter somewhere in the Leighton Buzzard area.

We set off downriver; as usual we set off later than intended. At Upper Barnwell I showed them how to operate the locks and between us we decided on a routine to get us down the Nene. Admittedly it wasn't a slick routine and it certainly wasn't a pretty routine. I was out of practice at manoeuvring a boat not having moved it for five months and they were novices at the getting on and off and operating locks but it sort of worked, sometimes. As an additional hazard the river was still flowing strongly and the water levels

91

were high. At Ashton Lock, when the guillotine gate was lowered the river flowed over the gates at each end and standing at the stern of the boat in the lock I had the illusion of being in an infinity pool.

We stopped at lovely Fotheringhay for the evening. We took too long next morning wandering around the pretty village where Richard III was born and the site of Fotheringhay Castle where Mary Queen of Scots was incarcerated and then beheaded. We spent an age looking in the church, which gave much information about both of the village's illustrious residents. Then after all that exertion we needed to have one more cup of coffee. It was nearly midday when we set off. Peterborough seemed to be getting further away rather than nearer.

As we approached the first lock, Warmington, we could see that somebody was lowering the guillotine gate. I assumed there was a boat coming through the lock, I couldn't see one so thought it must be a small boat. We decided that I'd moor up and the crew would go to help the boat through. I went into the lock landing a bit faster than usual to compensate for the cross wind and a strong pull from the by-water that flowed away to the right and over a weir. I over-compensated and No 1 Crew decided I was going too fast, didn't want to risk being catapulted onto the bank or into the river so promptly sat down instead of getting off. The wimp. I bounced off the lock landing and Rea was pulled across the river by the draw from the weir and the stiff breeze. Five minutes later after much huffing and puffing on my part and grinding and roaring on the part of the engine we got back onto the landing and tied up.

There was a woman operating the lock and gesticulating at us but I still couldn't see a boat in the lock and there was none in sight. Why? Did she enjoy a workout on the guillotine wheel? Did she have a lock fetish? Was she mad? The crew went warily forth to see what was happening. Dog-phobic No 2 Crew was not helped by the presence of two large black Labradors. 'They won't hurt you.' She said. That is what all devoted dog owners say when their beloved beasts are doing an unwanted slobber over a hapless passer-by.

No 2 crew was instructed by the Lady of the Lock to take the windlass and close the paddles. As an ex school head more used to giving orders than obeying orders she went into dumb mode, 'Windlass? Oh you mean this windy thing. What should I do with it?'

The crew opened the lock gates (both gates as instructed by the Lady of the Lock) and I pinged in. I wasn't having a good driving day. The Lady of the Lock took my bow rope and tied it to the bollard. I shouted to No 1 Crew and she untied, dropped it back onto the bow and took the centre rope and according to our now established, although still not pretty routine, she looped it round a bollard and passed the end back to me. There's no point in being tied securely in a lock when you have a crew that are prone to stand and chat or wander off to look at the wildlife totally ignoring the fact that the boat is tilting over side-ways and is in imminent danger of sinking. The v-gates closed the crew went to the wheel to raise the gate; being an isolated lock with no electricity supply Warmington Lock has a manual, not electric, wheel to operate the guillotine gate. By now the crew were used to the hard work of manual wheels as they already operated them at Ashton and Perio. Their system was to vigorously open it for a few minutes then collapse exhausted for another ten minutes, have a long chat then gradually, with much talking and resting between turns, wind the wheel the rest of the way. They were told off for doing it too quickly and letting the water out too rapidly. The Lady of the Lock obviously didn't realise that this vigorous burst of energy wouldn't last long. At this point she deemed my crew to be completely incompetent dismissed them and told them to wait on the lock landing while she finished opening the lock. Unexpectedly obedient they did so.

'Excuse me lady, might I need my rope unwrapping before my crew are dismissed?' So I sat in the deep lock: lock empty: gate open: no crew: Lady of the Lock looking into the distance and I was still attached to a bollard. I did a few ineffectual sweeps with the rope to try and unfasten it then I climbed on the roof to unwrap the rope and made my way back to the helm. Then I managed to drop the rope into the water and had to walk along the gunwale to retrieve it. After all that I went to collect my crew. 'What kept you? They asked. Yet they hadn't bothered to ask why a woman fully equipped with keys and windlass was operating a boat-less lock in the middle of nowhere. We still don't know why she was there.

By the time we arrived in Elton it was lunch-time and we had to go to the pub. Marcelle always feels it is obligatory to eat fish, chips and mushy peas when she is in England. Then when full of fish and chips and mushy peas, we got back to the boat it started to rain so I made the unsurprising decision not to go to Peterborough but to leave the boat in Elton. We got a lift back to Oundle to collect our respective cars and we all went off in different directions.

In view of all the rain we'd been having I'd moved the boat back into the lee of the river on the inside of a bend so the strong current passed it by. I re-enforced the pins which were hammered into the soft bank by re-arranging the ropes so that the additional centre and rear ropes were tied to trees and there was enough ply in the ropes to allow for the river to rise or fall by a couple of feet while I was away. It was a wise decision, in the three days that I was away the rain came down and the river went up. I did worry about the safety of the boat with all that water about so I rang the Man Who Knows Everything and he checked it, each day, on his way to and from work.

I re-joined the boat on a grey and wet afternoon and watched a swan's nest floating past. The wind was whipping in from the west, the boat was buffeted against the bank and when I got on board the interior felt cold and damp. I wished I'd stayed a few more days in London. Once again Strong Stream Advice had been issued so that meant I was stuck in Elton until it was lifted. What was becoming the usual suspects of trees, dead sheep, branches and fence posts passed by the port side of the boat; at one point a shed went merrily on its way before jamming against the weir. Over a period of time, it disintegrated and headed off in bits in the direction of Peterborough. It had also been a wise decision, even if it was due more to inertia than careful planning, not to go to Peterborough. The bankside in Peterborough is concrete and stepped and the mooring rings are on the lower steps. Wise boaters who were stranded at Peterborough hammered scaffold poles between their boats and the bank to stop their boats drifting nearer the bank as the river rose and flowed over the stepped concrete. This meant there was a wonderful array of cobbled-together gangplanks and escape routes along the quayside in Peterborough that enabled the inhabitants to get off their boats and onto the bank. When the river subsided suddenly it was the people with scaffold poles and wobbly gangplanks that were the winners. They may have had a challenging time getting on and off their boats for the previous three weeks and they may have lost the odd gangplank when the river went down but now their boats went down with the water and were safe. Boats that had risen with the river over the first few steps were suddenly left high and dry along on the concrete bank when the river levels fell suddenly. In more than one case the boats secured to the bank leant over, filled with water and sank. In Wansford a boat that had risen with the river and floated above the bank was left marooned in a back garden and it was months before it could be re-floated.

I was stuck at Elton for three weeks. It continued to rain, not as heavily as it had in the previous months, but the already sodden ground could not absorb any more water.

Despite the high level and strong flow of the river I was tied securely at a point where the water did not seem to be in danger of flooding over the bank. I gave up on the gangplank as I could not get it placed safely across the long stretch from my boat onto the soft bank. My method of getting on and off the boat was to walk along the gunwale until I had reached the centre where the boat was nearest the bank then I lowered myself onto the bank and went on my way. Getting on was a reverse of this procedure and meant leaning towards the boat, catching the top rail and then striding over the gap between boat and bank and shuffling back along the gunwale. Not a difficult procedure in daylight but a bit dodgier in the dark, especially if I had left my head torch behind when I'd gone out. There was a cruiser alongside me but the crew, wisely, spent most evenings in the pub so if I fell in I'd have been by myself and nobody would hear me scream. I know from bitter experience that it's not the falling in that's the problem it's the getting out. I did hear my neighbour fall in late one evening, a big splash followed by a lot of shouting but by the time I'd found my dressing gown and shoes and gone out to help they were safely back on their boat, one or both of them drying out.

The water bounced over the weir, the floating lock pontoon which rose when the river rose couldn't get any higher and was completely submerged. At night the noise of the river falling over the weir drowned out all other night time noises, the call of the owls, the harsh bark of the fox and the occasional night time grumble of the calves in the field alongside me. The only noise that out-vocalised the sound of gushing water was the noise from any object that got trapped under the boat. Even small items trapped under the boat reverberate against the steel and cause a loud banging. I was often woken in the night by what sounded like enthusiastic hammering. It was disturbing to hear an object large enough to sink the Titanic banging against the hull. When the eddy of the water eventually released the culprit, it was rather disappointing to see it was just a small log.

On a mild night when there was a full moon I wrapped myself in a blanket and took a glass of wine and sat in the bow to watch the river flow past. A river in spate is fascinating to watch and when a full moon turns the water into a silvery shimmer and black unidentifiable objects come hurtling around the bend breaking the texture of the bright, mottled silver surface it is hypnotic. I sat for an age watching the water stream past until the night air became too chilly and the wine glass became too empty.

So basically I was okay at Elton. As the flood water subsided I was able to go for long walks over sodden and silent fields, I had my car nearby if I needed anything and had my neighbours to talk to. I offered to shop for them but they mostly preferred to get local buses and explore the area, a sensible move if you are stranded somewhere: take the opportunity to get to know the area. When they were running short of water the EA drove up with large containers and filled their water tank.

By the time Strong Stream Advice was lifted I'd changed my mind about going to Ely and Cambridge, I still had it in my mind that I'd be going onto the canal system this year and Cambridge was in the wrong direction so I turned around and went back to Oundle. The Man Who Knows Everything came to help me back through the locks. The river still had a strong flow on it but it is easier, albeit slower, going against the flow than with it. I did manage to take a chunk of Fotheringhay Bridge with me but there again I often take a chunk of Fotheringhay bridge with me even if the river is like a millpond. The Man Who Knows Everything had brought cans of lager for himself and cans of cider for me. I thought what a pleasant and helpful person he was, by the time I'd finished my third can of cider I was even beginning to think he was good-looking as well, then I looked at the label and saw that the cider was 8 percent proof. That explained it, I didn't open the fourth can of cider I had a cup of coffee instead.

Off Again

June 3rd was the day of the Thames River Pageant for Queen's Diamond Jubilee when over a thousand boats sailed as a flotilla down the Thames. The wind blew and the rain fell and one of the abiding images of the event was the choir from the Royal College of Music singing their hearts out whilst looking like drowned rats. Despite the weather, and the crowds, I wish I'd made the effort to see that parade, I'm not a Royalist but I am a boatist and would have loved to see a thousand boats of every conceivable shape and vintage making their way down the Thames. Earlier in the year I'd been working in Richmond and had watched the rowers practising in the ornately decorated rowboat Gloriana. It was pouring with rain that day as well but on that occasion the rowers weren't wearing the full gold and red regalia they were prepared for the weather and dressed in orange kagools. On the day of the parade orange kagools were obviously not deemed suitable attire to wear before the Queen but all that sodden red and gold must have been uncomfortable and they must have wished for some sensible wet weather clothing.

Instead of standing in the rain watching boats go past I had given up on my plan to move onto the canal system and was making a second attempt to get to Ely and beyond. I'd joined a feeble imitation of the Royal flotilla and travelled down to Peterborough with three other boats going to a boater's rally. I intended to stay at the rally for a couple of days then carry on through the Fens and join the Great Ouse and pootle around there for about two months meeting up with friends and enjoying some warm dry summer weather on a riverbank. I was looking forward to riverside BBQ's; sitting on the bank in the sunshine reading my book; leisurely cruises along the river. I'm an optimist.

The journey started well, our small group set off in the evening and stopped at Fotheringhay for the requisite visit to the Falcon Inn. The following morning the weather was good although the weather forecast wasn't. The sun shone on us but ominous black clouds sat on the horizon to the west. As we untied the boats fat lambs and their mothers lined up on the hummock that had been the execution place of Mary Queen of Scots and watched us with expressionless yellow eyes. The trees and bushes still had the myriad green tones of late spring. White swathes of cow parsley and the pink of early dog roses lined the banks. When I passed bushes of elderflower their heavy scent filled the sunlit air. At Elton Lock a flock of yellow wagtails pecked at the stone of the lock-side. At Nassington a kaleidoscope of parachutes fell from the sky in front of us. Large yellow and frilly white water-lilies floated on the surface of the river. Beyond Elton where the disused water mill stood sentient behind the lock

101

the big yellow water-lilies were superseded by more delicate water-lilies with a single pink flower on a long stem. Swallows darted across the surface of the water, when the sun caught them their backs changed from dark blue to an iridescent indigo. Above us red kites wheeled and called, too high above for me to be able to discern the colour of their chestnut wings or their white underbellies. Beyond Yarwell I was admiring the smart development of new houses and trying to peer in the windows to see their furnishings when I realised I had left the river and headed off down a small creek. I reversed out and picked up the route of the river and arrived at the next lock where my travelling companion was already in the lock waiting for me, wondering what had delayed me.

Our floating idyll lasted as far as Alwalton when the black clouds that had been building up and following us caught up. We'd been taking a zig-zag route along the meandering river and they'd taken the direct route across the fields. The forecasted rain arrived warning us to put on water-proofs by first splattering the boat roof with big splodges of water then settling down to a steady downpour.

The rain is a not a respecter of rank. Rain is not just for the royals, it didn't just pour down on the Queen's parade it poured down for the rest of the weekend on our rally as well. The field where the marquee was erected became a quagmire and events were cancelled, we needed to don wellies to get to the bar and if you sat on chairs the legs were apt to sink into the mud leaving the top of the table at eye level. For the concert evening our sketch featuring a King

Canute trying to stop the waters of the Nene rising became appropriate. The Magical Mechanic, who was playing the part of King Canute had an accent that started off in Denmark and then wandered through Ireland and Pakistan before coming to a halt somewhere near Birmingham. I think it's best he doesn't give up the day job.

It was obvious to the boaters who had spent years on this river that flood measures would once again be put in place. Many boats left early to travel up stream before the river was closed. I re-arranged my passage through Stanground Lock and left a day earlier than intended to go downriver. The strength of the river was apparent when I tried to turn the boat. Plan A didn't work when I couldn't turn the bow against the flow of the river, Plan B meant reversing into a backwater and letting the flow whapp my bow around.

Alongside Orton Lock there is a strong weir where poles are set as a slalom course for white water rafting. The water was turbulent and even the canoeists had decided it wasn't safe to come out to play. I left the lock and then didn't have enough power to outrun the pull of the water and was headed on a collision course with another narrowboat waiting on the lock landing. At the last minute the water pulled me in a different direction and a collision was averted. As the flood waters again rose behind me and Strong Stream Advice was issued and the locks were reversed I reached the calm of the dykes and drainage ditches of the Middle Levels. I headed towards Salters Lode Lock where there is a short tidal stretch of the Great Ouse to negotiate before going through the large Denver Lock and onto the non-tidal stretch of the river.

103

I had booked my transition through Salters Lode Lock and I moored up in this isolated spot on the Fens to wait for the tide to turn. I'd done this half mile passage twice before and hadn't had any problems, well except for being under the impression that the turn to Denver was to the left and not to the right. This time there was the additional hazard that sandbanks had formed in the channel and it was now impossible to moor up on the tidal stretch outside Denver Lock. The passage between the two locks had to be carefully calibrated by the lock keepers so that boats passed in the middle of the stretch and neither had to go near the formidable sandbanks. I waited for the high tide to arrive. The first boat, a cruiser went out without a problem and the first boat from Denver passed him in mid-stream and came in. Then it was my turn. The tide had turned and was going out and I got my instructions: I had to carry on up the river, the lock keeper at Denver would be on the bridge and would signal when I had to make the turn along the edge of the sand bank and into the lock entrance. 'That current looks strong,' I said to the lock keeper. 'Mmmm...' he said in a non-committal manner with a half grin on his face.

As I was leaving the lock he shouted down to me, 'as soon as your stern is clear of the sandbank, gun it.' I had no time to think that that sounded an ominous warning I just followed instructions and as soon as my stern was clear I put on full power and 'gunned it'. I was now travelling faster than I usually travelled but I was going downstream instead of upstream, the current had caught me and I was travelling broadside along the wide Great Ouse towards Kings Lynn. On full throttle and with the tiller pushed hard to the left I still seemed to be losing the fight with the strong current. Rea's nose was getting dangerously close to the muddy bank as she refused to turn more than 90 degrees. Feelings of panic were starting to rise. Visions of spending the next day stranded on a muddy bank were starting to form. As the nose almost reached the bank I was suddenly out of the strongest flow of water. Gradually, gradually Rea's nose came around. I was well out of sight of Salter's Lode before I eventually turned her into the current and was able to make my way back towards Denver. As I passed the watchers on the lock I did my best regal wave and got a cheer in response.

Then the next obstacle was the large sandbank that was obstructing the entrance to Denver Lock. I tried to do as I was told and waited until I got the signal to turn left and then come in between the wall of the sluice gates and the sandbank. The problem was that there was a row of people on the bridge above the lock and my eyesight isn't good enough to discern which one was the lock keeper. When I did identify him he was frantically jumping up and down and making circular signals in the air. I think he was telling me to turn urgently. I did a quick turn, bounced off the stanchions to the sluices and got into the lock safely. To the amusement of the lock-side watchers I then got a lecture on not obeying instructions and wasting peoples time. His statement, 'You're not the only boat that wants to come through on this tide,' being repeated frequently.

I tied up outside the Jennyns Arms feeling in need of a large glass of wine. Sitting in the garden admiring the view across the wide expanse of water the man from the boat that came out of Salters Lode after me came over for a chat.

'I got caught by the current as well,' he told me, 'but I managed it better than you. I only travelled a few yards before I got her turned.'

Oh, I just love competitive boating.

I didn't point out that his boat was shorter than mine and he had a bow thruster I just took a sip of wine, smiled sweetly and said, 'You're obviously a very experienced boater.'

'I like to think I know what I'm doing,' he said, failing to notice the hint of sarcasm in my voice and the gleam of malice in my eyes.

Schadenfreude Saturday 1

The narrow, bendy, weedy Old West River leaves the wide Great Ouse at Pope's Corner and runs for just over eleven miles to Hermitage Lock at Earith where once again the river becomes known as the Great Ouse.

I'd overnighted at the Lazy Otter moorings at Stretham and Karen has joined me for the ride to St Ives.

We don't see another boat for a few miles then an impatient cruiser, which had been moored behind me at Streham, catches up with us. He is probably furious with himself because he hadn't made it off the moorings ahead of us. If I had a river cruiser I would have been annoyed as well; a narrowboat moves so much more slowly than a cruiser and on this shallow, bendy river it is often difficult to over-take a slow mover. This cruiser is new and bright white; an expensive bit of kit. In contrast to his bright, white boat the new owner is bright red in the face with apoplexy because he has got stuck behind this damn narrowboat. He probably thinks narrowboats should stick to the canals and not come along clogging up the rivers. He drives close behind me, tooting his horn every so often just to remind me he is there, as if I hadn't noticed that a white bow was poking alongside my stern every few minutes. I'm not being awkward (for once) if there had been an opportunity to move aside to let him pass I would have done so. After Twentypence Bridge there are two wide sweeping bends, I know from bitter experience that when the river levels are low there are shoals on the outer parts of the bends so I follow the ruffles on the water that denote the deeper part and take the wider route; following the river's flow and avoiding shoals. He had been about to overtake and is so infuriated by me driving wide around the bends that he keeps his hand hard on the horn, shattering the peace of this quiet morning. At the next curve I keep to the outside of the bend where the water is deepest and he sees his opportunity to over-take, puts on full throttle, gives me a two-fingered salute as he passes me and then promptly grinds to a halt on a shoal. As I pass him I return his two-fingered salute and chug on my way. Karen is laughing happily by my side. Had the circumstances been different I would have offered help, a tow maybe or at the least a few kind words. In this case I just take quiet pleasure from his predicament.

It isn't until we reach the GOBA (Great Ouse Boating Association) moorings at Aldreth that he once more catches up with us. No tooting of the horn this time, he seems to be more subdued. Anyway neither of us are going anywhere because as we round the bend there is a narrowboat jammed crossways across the river and blocking it. The two crew members are trying to turn a fifty-foot boat in a forty-eight-foot wide river and, unsurprisingly, it has got stuck.

The woman is on the bank heaving at the bow rope the man is at the tiller revving the engine for all it is worth (they don't care it's only a hire boat) and the boat is firmly embedded. The bow is hard against the pilings and the stern is stuck securely in the reeds. He shouts at us not to come too close, probably thinking 'we haven't seen a boat come past all day, now I'm looking stupid two come along at once.'

All the revving and pulling is to no avail, the stern is still firmly stuck and the bow seems to be even more tightly jammed against the pilings. I, and the cruiser behind me, hover in the river keeping out of their way. The crew of the stuck boat swap places, she sits at the stern revving the engine he goes to stand on the riverbank pulling at the bow rope. He is panicking, it's bad enough getting your boat stuck but getting it stuck with an audience! He leans over to pull at a different angle and falls in the river.

I'm not laughing, honest I'm not laughing and my crew-mate Karen isn't laughing either, really she isn't laughing. As a frequent faller-inner I have a great deal of sympathy with him. Honestly, it's not at all funny. In addition, he has fallen with one leg in the river and one between the pilings and the bank which probably means he has hurt himself and definitely means he is going to have a problem getting out. Eventually he emerges dripping from the river and recommences the tugging at the bow rope. We're still not laughing, honest we're not.

I tell Karen to compose herself and go to the front of our boat to ask if they'd like a push. The lady says 'yes please,' so I move Rea forward and manoeuvre her so she is gently pushing against the side of their boat. That doesn't work. I reverse, give a lot more throttle and hit their boat on the side, nearer the stern this time and with a good thump. The woman in the other boat almost falls off her seat and has to grab hold of the tiller to stop herself becoming the second, soggy casualty of the day but suddenly like a cork from a champagne bottle they are released from the reed bed. The man pulls the bow forward, leaving us enough space to squeeze through. We wave cheerily and go on our way leaving him to dry off and regain some dignity.

The river cruiser uses the fact that I am now slowly scraping along in the reed bed to overtake me on the wrong side at a bend and steams off into the distance creating enough wake to disturb every nesting bird in Cambridgeshire. Huhhh....

Schadenfreude Saturday 2

It's early evening at Clayhithe and there are voices on the towpath, shouts from the river and sounds of a general kerfuffle so I put down my book and go outside to see what's happening. A narrowboat is sideways across the river and a wide-beam boat is drifting away downstream. There is a certain amount of shouted instructions passing between them. It appears that the narrowboat is attempting to moor up but has no engine and therefore no power. It has arrived with a tow from the wide-beam but, somehow, they have become separated.

One thing a lone woman on a boat is never short of is advice: advice from men. This predicament gives me a chance to get my own back and give a lot of unwanted and unheeded instructions to a male boater having difficulty. I stand on the bank with the inhabitants of the other moored boats and join in the shouting of suggestions; suggestions that are likely to be inaudible to the crews of the boats and will most certainly be ignored even if they do hear them.

While my good advice is being ignored I get into conversation with a woman who has some connection with the boats. We both know exactly what they should do, if the whole scheme had been left to women instead of put in the hands of incompetent men they'd all be safely moored and the crews would be having a drink in The Bridge pub. In fact it's not just boats but the world in general would be a better and more efficient and kinder place if women were left to run it; (Margaret Thatcher is excluded from this scenario). Once we have set all the woes of the world to rights we return to the problem of how to get the boat tethered to the shore. We both decide all the stranded boat needs to do is throw a rope ashore.

A man on the towpath has read our thoughts. 'Throw me the rope,' he shouts to the man on the boat. The man on the boat scrambles around on the roof and finds a rope. The rope is duly thrown. One end lands limply on the tow path while the other end falls in the water

'You bloody idiot you were meant to tie one end of the rope to the boat,' he shouts.

The bloody idiot pointedly turns his back on the towpath contingent, lights a cigarette and waits patiently for the breeze and flow of the river to take him where it will.

The Little Ouse

I had intended to return to the Nene in the middle of July and then head over to the canal system for a couple of months but the rains and the floods continued. Three times I was on The Great Ouse heading towards Denver when I got notification that Strong Stream Advice had been issued for the Nene. On the first occasion I had left the boat at Little Thetford and gone to London for a few days to visit my daughter. I was hardly off the train at Kings Cross when I received a text notification that flood notices had been issued between Cambridge and Ely. I rang the EA to ask how much danger there was to boats, only to get an ear bashing from the river inspector for leaving my boat alone in an isolated spot. I think that was the only time in my years on the boat that the EA or C&RT were anything other than polite, friendly and helpful. I was unsure of how tightly I had tied Rea; maybe I hadn't left enough slack in the ropes to allow for the rising of this wide, apparently benign river whose levels I hadn't expected to fluctuate much. I returned to the boat the next day. She was fine and the river levels didn't seem a lot higher but I suppose it was worth checking as I would have been a bit upset if she'd sank with all my worldly goods on board.

On the third occasion when I was heading towards Denver and yet again advised that the Nene was closed I decide on a change of scenery and I did a detour and went down the Little Ouse to Brandon. I found it a peaceful, rural cruise. After I'd passed the two miles of linear moorings at Brandon Creek I saw no other boats. Crops of wheat ready to be harvested were alternated with fallow ploughed fields, the black soil of the Fens glinting moistly in the sunlight. The bare fields gave off the tang of damp, peaty earth which was interspersed with a sweet heady perfume when I passed a field of beans, a smell that reminded me of the Nivea hand-cream my mother used. Where cows and calves grazed the water meadows and came down into the glutinous hollows along the river to drink the smell was of cow dung. In the one field a herd of picturesque Highland Cattle supping at the water's edge were particularly pungent. There were rickety farm buildings and in the distance a flock of seagulls could be seen following a tractor but otherwise the day was devoid of habitation, people and boats. The spires of Cambridge sitting mistily on the horizon to my right had a fairy tale quality.

On an isolated stretch, the river meandered between banks awash with rosebay willow herb and the white flowers of bindweed. Reeds and grasses grew densely down to the water's edge to meet the yellow flowers of water lilies. The only disturbance to the tranquillity of the day was the jets that intermittently came over very low and very loud to land at the nearby American airbase at Lakenheath. The sudden loud roar, with the plane seemingly only feet overhead, frightened the living daylights out of me but the grazing cattle took no notice whatsoever; screeching jets must just be part of their daily routine. Droves of blue and black damselflies accompanied the boat and the usual contingent of cormorants, herons and geese littered the bank side. The weather on the Fens plays a major part in the enjoyment of the countryside because the huge open skies are such an integral part of the landscape. When the wind is from the east, the sky can be flat and murky for days on end and the result is drabness and depression. For my journey down Brandon Creek a warm southerly breeze sent the sun scuttling in and out amongst fluffy white clouds and the air was alive with the buzzing of insects and the swallows that swooped to catch them.

I made my way gently down the Little Ouse towards Brandon. Consulting the map I could see it was navigable almost into the town centre so I thought I'd try and moor there. I put Rea into the only lock on the river but looking behind I couldn't see how I was going to close the gate. I checked my guide again and saw that the lock was only forty-five-foot long so I took sixty-foot Rea out and headed towards a short pontoon which had mooring space. The pontoon and the river were cluttered with boys (and one girl) and their paraphernalia enjoying one of the rare days of warm, sunny weather in this wet summer. I didn't want to spoil their games by taking up all the pontoon so moored with the stern against the pontoon and put pins in to tie the bow to the bank. Where boys are concerned it's usually best not to spoil their fun, thereby incurring their wrath. Boys around boats are lovely and inquisitive and helpful when they're on your side and a bloody nightmare when they've taken against you.

After I'd tied up I said hello to the boys and one of them wandered over to ask if they could borrow my boat pole so they could test the depth of the water. I lifted it off the roof and handed it down to them and they spent a happy hour swimming around passing it to each other and poking it into the riverbed to see where the deepest part was. Luckily nowhere appeared to be deep so they didn't lose my boat pole, although I think the loss of the boat pole was what they were hoping for so they could then heroically dive for it. Bored with calibrating the depth of the river they asked if they could jump in from the roof of my boat. I said, 'No', I'd prefer not to have bloodstains on my boat if they miss-jumped but they could jump in from the stern. From inside I could feel the boat rocking as they climbed on the stern and jumped in but that game soon became boring as well so they went back to their fishing rods and nets.

I locked the boat and went for a stroll into the town, first extracting a promise from the boys that they wouldn't go jumping off the roof of my boat. They promised fervently that they wouldn't jump off the roof and promised equally as fervently that they would look after my boat while I was gone. I chose to believe them. I walked down the riverbank in the direction of Brandon, stopping to talk to a woman with dripping wet hair and an undefinable aura of oddness about her who told me she has lived here all her life and comes down to the river to swim most days, winter and summer. 'Isn't it very cold in the winter?' I asked her.

116

'Oh I don't take my clothes off in the winter.' I had a vision of her swimming in a thick coat, woolly gloves and a hat. The boys had already established that the river is not deep so if she became waterlogged and sank I suppose she'd still be able to walk out.

By the time I got back to the boat it was the evening and the boys were still messing about on the river but in a quieter, more subdued manner. One of them came over to ask me questions about the boat and asked if he could see the engine. I lifted the floor boards to show him the engine. 'Wow,' he said. He called two of his mates over and they climbed on the stern and peered down at the engine. 'Wow,' they said. I peered down at my engine. I had never thought it had the 'Wow factor.' Looking at the grimy and oily lump of metal I was still not wowed. Maybe being impressed with engines is a male thing. They asked intelligent questions about the workings of the boat and I explained as best I could, until the questions become too technical.

'Yes I can have a shower, I have a bathroom and a gas boiler provides hot water or if the engine is running I have a calorifier.'

'What's a calorifier?'

'It's something that heats the water when the engine is running.'

'Yes but what is it and how does it work?'

'I'm not sure.'

'But it's your boat so you must know how it works.'

'Well I run the engine and in an hour I have hot water, that's all I need to know. OK'

'But……..'

There was a shout from the bank. 'Aaron your mother is looking for you and she says if you're not home in ten minutes you're grounded.'

'Oh shit,' said the boy I assumed to be Aaron and he shot off to gather bike, clothes and fishing equipment from the bushes and disappeared into the gathering dusk. The remaining boys gathered up their belongings and followed in hot pursuit. Calm and quietness descended on the riverbank.

I was just pouring the first glass of wine when there was a knock on the roof. It was the swimming lady I'd spoken to earlier and she'd brought me a bag of walnuts and a selection of religious pamphlets. She hoped I'd enjoy the nuts, read the pamphlets and think deeply about the message from Jesus. So that's what her aura of oddness was: religion.

I left the mooring early the next morning, before boys or religious swimmers were about, and headed back towards Ely to meet up with my sister who was flying over from Italy. We had intended to go up the Nene and onto the canal system but because of the high river levels that wasn't going to happen, so it was to be a few days in Ely and Cambridge and then hopefully, if the Nene was open I would have her company along the boring stretch of the Middle Levels and help with the locks through to Oundle.

Sandbanks

It was my birthday. I'd picked up my sister in Ely a few days earlier and we were at Denver. The following day we planned to go through the two locks, onto the Middle Levels and then make our way gradually up the Nene. Two friends had joined us for a birthday BBQ and we were on the riverbank, the sun was warm, the wine was cold and the sausages were burning gently when a man walked along the flood bank and shouted down to us. 'Do you know that Denver Lock is closed for the next five days?'

I chose not to believe him. I had another glass of wine and some more food and I was feeling mellow until another passer-by confirmed what the first had said and destroyed my complacency. I went to the lock to enquire about the closure. It would seem that in this year of wet feet, stranded boats and plans constantly thwarted by rain, floods and rising rivers the lock at Denver would be closed for up to five days because of lack of water. The sandbanks that had formed at the entrance to the lock were now causing a blockage. The EA were working on them but the lack of progress was coupled with the fact that there were mean tides over the next few days when the high-water level was predicted to be comparatively low. There was no possibility of boats passing through the lock for at least three days. We would have to wait until the fuller moon brought the higher spring tides to send more water into the narrow channel next to the sand banks and enable boats to have enough depth to transit.

I went back to my birthday celebrations and more friends arrived and we adjourned to the pub for dinner. Denver is an interesting place to visit for a day, but not for five days so during the course of the evening my sister and I managed to book a hotel and checked train and bus times. We were going to the sea-side.

The moorings at Denver are only for 48-hours but as the lock was closed I didn't think that I would be prosecuted for over-staying. We set off the next morning to walk to Downham Market to catch the train to Kings Lynn. I could have gone through the other lock at Denver and along the channel for a mile and moored at Downham Market but that took too much organisation on a morning after celebrating my birthday, it just seemed easier to walk and I hoped it would help clear my head.

We pushed our way through a group of horses clustered around the gate to the footpath and set off along the high flood bank to walk to the train station at Downham Market. I was keeping a wary eye out for cows. I don't mind pushing horses aside but I have in my mind the number of walkers trampled to death by cows (twelve in the last few years) and I became nervous about approaching the group ahead of us on the pathway. I was preparing to scramble down the bank and fight my way through a mass of bramble bushes rather than walk through the herd but Marcelle said I was being stupid and walked calmly amongst them. I took a deep breath and followed; they were young cattle and barely lifted their heads from their grazing. I think it is cows with calves that can be dangerous but I prefer to err on the side of caution and avoid all cattle at all times. The walk took longer than we had expected and we arrived at Downham Market station just in time to see our train leave. The small Railway Arms, a Brief Encounter type bar and café on the station platform, was closed, which was a pity because I'd heard good things about it. We decided to kill time seeing the sights of Downham Market. I estimated that it wouldn't take any longer than the hour we had to waste to savour all the delights the town had to offer. I have driven along the A10 towards Kings Lynn and seen the brown sign to this historic market town (every market town in England has a brown sign saying it's historic) but I'd never left the main road to visit it. I didn't do much of a visit this time either, we never got beyond the Crown Inn, a lovely oak panelled pub with a fabulous staircase. We were impressed with the pub and so intent on listening to the local clientele's lovely Norfolk accents, with vowels that stretched into infinity, that we had to break into a jog to get back to the station in time to catch the next train. From a distance the market square with its quirky black and white clock tower did appear to be worth a longer look: maybe on the way back I'll visit it properly.

Five days later, after a great time walking the coastal paths, eating fish and viewing seals, Marcelle headed back to

Italy. I arrived back at Denver to find squatters on my boat. In my absence spiders had colonised it, every window had four spiders merrily abseiling up and down. Their webs and lines neatly spaced to give each a defined territory. There were spiders on the ceiling in the bedroom and across the mirror in the bathroom. On the plus side there weren't any flies or mosquitos about. I don't care for big, hairy, long legged spiders but I'm quite fond of these smaller, square shaped, short-legged spiders that take up residence on boats. I have been advised that horse-chestnuts deter spiders and have noticed that many boats have a line of horse chestnuts on the window sills. An old wife's tale? There does seem to be insect sprays on the market that contain horse chestnut extract so maybe there is some truth in it. As it is there aren't any horse chestnut trees in the vicinity so I just collected the most inconvenient of the residents and put them outside then left the rest of them alone to, hopefully, feast on any visiting mosquitoes.

I was told the lock would be re-opened on that afternoon's tide. The first boats out had an audience, ranged along the road bridge above the lock, leaning over the parapets, waiting to watch them leave. The opinions as to what the Environment Agency should be doing about the sand banks which were causing a delay to this batch of boaters, who all had better things to do with their time than hang around at Denver, were varied. The most imaginative was to get the fire-brigade in to train their hoses on the sand banks to disperse them. I happened to be standing next to a water engineer who explained the problem in a more measured manner. The sand bank that had formed outside the lock gate and was blocking the lock landing had been building gradually for some time but had only become a real problem this year. The heavy rainfall during the winter washed a lot of silt down from the Old Bedford River, which is tidal for twenty miles to the lock at Brownshill Staunch, (although the rise and fall is slight once it reaches the Great Ouse again). If the sand bank were to be dismantled the water would take the silt and simply move the problem elsewhere. That sounded logical to me for you don't have to be on a boat for long to be aware of the power, the determination and the pure bloody-mindedness of water.

Two cruisers left the lock first and their manoeuvrability, size and shallow draft made the exit look easy. The first narrowboat, a fifty-footer went next and after a lot of shouting between the crew and some judicious use of the boat pole by the crew member standing on the bow they got through. A narrowboat from Salters Lode came upriver and got into the lock effortlessly but the next boat to leave, a sixty-foot narrowboat, got his bow stuck on the bank and ended up reversing back into the lock so he could wait until the next day when the tide would be fractionally higher and the yellow digger may have chipped away a bit more sandbank.

I decided I wouldn't go on the early tide I'd watch boats make the passage through and then see if it was safe to go on the afternoon tide.

By the time I got off my boat the next day, it was too late to watch the morning boats leaving. The news was filtering down the line of moored boats that a hire boat trying to leave on the early tide had got stuck on the sand bank. I went to look: the tide had receded and a Fox's hire boat was sitting high and dry on the mud. The curtains were closed but laughter drifted up from the boat. Evidently it was a party of young men on the boat and they seemed to be determined to enjoy themselves whatever the circumstances. I hoped the beer didn't run out before they were re-floated.

All of us watchers gathered for the evening tide to see an employee of Fox's, shipped out to the stranded boat, spend half an hour revving, shuffling, revving, reversing, churning up mud and water and eventually getting the boat off the bank and on its way back to their base at March.

There were no more boats leaving that evening. I decided to go the next day.

The next day it was raining. I'd wait until the following day.

Then the following day arrived and I could no longer put off the time when I had to leave. I moved over to the lock landing and it was decided I would be the second of the three sixty-foot narrowboats that were planning to make the journey. They both had crew and bow-thrusters and they were nervous. I was alone and I was very nervous. I'm not sure what use a crew member would be apart from mopping my fevered brow but I did covert their bow-thrusters because a bow-thruster would enable me to turn much more sharply out of the entrance. I'd never wanted a bow thruster before because I've always thought that they were just one more thing to go wrong. I wanted one then.

124

The first boat left with no problems. The lock-keeper, who in the past had moaned at me for turning up late and not being quick enough into the lock was kind and encouraging and gave helpful advice. I left the lock with a pounding heart and went nearer the sand bank than I had intended but still got out without a problem. I motored down to Salters Lode and turned perfectly into the lock. The Gods of Accurate Steering were smiling down on me that day.

The lock-keeper at Salters Lode was impressed with my smooth entry. 'Do you have a bow-thruster?' he asked.

'No. I don't need one,' I told him.

I'm often congratulated on my boat handling skills but it's not because I'm exceptionally good at handling a boat, it's because a lone woman handling a long boat is a bit like a dog walking on its hind legs; it's not that it's being done well rather that it's been done at all.

The whole procedure of getting through the locks safely had traumatised me and put an end to my boating for the day. I couldn't be bothered to ring Marston Priory to book a slot through the lock. I could get as far as Upwell but I couldn't be sure there would be a space on the short landing, my two travelling companions had gone on ahead and I decided they would probably take up the limited space on the thirty-six-hour mooring. That day the wind was strong, the next day the weather forecast was good: warm, calm and sunny. I got out the book and the wine and settled down for the rest of the day, only stirring myself to give words of wisdom to boaters who were arriving and planning to traverse the short stretch of tidal waters and do battle with the sandbanks the next day.

I listened to myself telling my tales of venturing out alone onto the tidal waters and thought it was amazing how hazardous I could make a mile of placid water seem and what an intrepid, fearless traveller I had become in the space of one short day.

March and Beyond

The following day I set off for March. The weather forecast was good but the weather wasn't. Instead of the promised warm and sunny morning, the day was overcast with a steady, drizzling rain. I couldn't put off the journey any longer as I was meeting a friend in Peterborough a couple of days later so I donned waterproof clothing and set off for the six-hour journey. There is a theory that there is no such thing as bad weather only bad clothing. I was wearing bad clothing. My waterproofs were no longer waterproof. In addition, it was warm and the humidity was high so underneath the leaky water-proofing I was sweating profusely thereby making me wetter inside the garments than it was outside.

The journey was tedious with frequent stops to clear weed from the prop. Four times I virtually ground to a halt and had to stop, remove the heavy hatch cover and lay down on my stomach tugging, pulling and swishing around with the bread knife at the tangle of weed that enveloped the propeller. As I passed the long linear villages of Upwell and Outwell the water was so shallow and clogged that I slowed almost to a halt and I was over-taken by old ladies, trundling shopping trollies, on the pathway next to the river. As I neared March the tops of the endless array of wind turbines stood motionless in the still, clammy air, the tops of their sails invisible in the low cloud. I went to free the prop of weed yet again and as I leant forward my new Smart phone dropped out of the top pocket of my non-waterproofs and landed with a splash in the bilges. I was glad to reach March. I went to a local shop and bought myself a child's fishing net and used it to fish my phone out of the bilge. Unsurprisingly, once removed from the oily gunge at the bottom of the bilge, the phone had died but at least the SIM card worked in my old phone. I was quite pleased to have my old, clunky phone back, it had survived being run over by a lorry, dropped countless times and on two occasions it had landed in the toilet. It would have had the stamina to survive a few hours in my bilge, unlike this wimpy newcomer. I didn't like my new phone anyway; it wasn't as smart as it thought it was because it was far too complicated to use. Or maybe it was just the operator that wasn't as smart as she thought she was.

In the evening I took advantage of being in a town and went to the launderette. There was one other customer; a young man slumped dejectedly on a bench watching an overfull machine clank painfully through its cycle occasionally depositing a spurt of soapy water on the floor.

I came over all mummsy and told him that he had too many clothes in one machine and he should have used two machines for that size of wash. 'But that would have cost a fortune,' he said. Then he lent against the seat and went back to watching the over-loaded machine go whirrrr bump, whirrrr bump, whirrr bump squirt, gave a deep sigh and said, 'I should never have left home.'

Back on the boat I enjoyed watching the geese on the bank opposite. There were eight of them; fat white geese, the edible variety that would roast beautifully accompanied by a tart gooseberry sauce to counteract their fattiness. They marched in line along the bottom of the steep bank and when a dog went past, or a cyclist splashed through a puddle on the pavement above them they all turned their heads upwards and in unison squawked loudly and aggressively at the passer-by. With the noise they were making, the traffic crossing the road bridge a few yards above me and the grating, clanking of the clock on the town hall I was not expecting a peaceful night. Later the traffic eased and the clock was turned off but nobody switched off the geese and they continued to be noisily vocal throughout the night.

The following day dawned bright and clear. We were getting the weather that was forecast for yesterday and there was no sign of the light rain that was forecast for today. Life in the Fens is in a bit of a time-warp, so maybe they always get their weather a day late. I left March in the early morning sunshine, fighting my way through overhanging willow trees, hoping that when blinded by the branches I didn't demolish one of the little cruisers moored at the bottom of the gardens. When I passed the Middle Level Commissioners' building, two yellow weed cutters set off in pursuit of me. Looking back from my position on the stern, I could only see the wide-open cutting jaws, their drivers invisible behind them. The weed cutters looked threatening as they followed me at a steady pace; in their apparently driverless state there was the suggestion of a manic machine about them. If I'd been blessed with anything other than a rudimentary imagination, I would have been convinced that they would suddenly spring forward and start to gnaw away at the stern of my boat devouring the metal chomp by chomp. I decided to ignore their presence and stared determinedly ahead of me down the straight, straight waterway and then when I did look back to check that they weren't gaining on me I found they'd gone. Logic told me I must have passed the entrance to one of the other drainage ditches without noticing it and they'd disappeared down there, but it still seemed eerie the way one minute they were menacingly behind me and the next minute they were nowhere to be seen.

The weed cutters must have already been along this stretch of ditch for the water was weed-free and clear. I could see down into the depths and watch the fish swimming amongst the reeds and underwater grasses. The blanket weed billowed under the water, serene dark clouds moving sensuously with the flow. Above and behind me two terns followed in my wake diving for the fish I had disturbed. Each time they dived they came up with a small silvery fish in their beak. I started to wonder how many fish a tern can eat but when I turned again to watch them, like the weed-cutters, they were no longer there.

As the morning wore on it got hot, I left the boat to float aimlessly and dived into the galley to get a glass of water and a hat. The problem on this stretch of the Middle Levels is that there is nowhere to stop and tie up and I'm wary of letting the boat rest on the bank in case I'm then stuck in a patch of reeds or in shallow water. For a man the need to empty the bladder can be dealt with easily, for a woman it is more of a problem, so when I set off for a journey that I know will take a few hours without a break I don't drink much before I leave. Then on a day like today when the sun burns down dehydration threatens.

I coughed my way through clouds of dust produced by a combine harvester hidden behind the flood bank and plodded on towards Whittlesey, the only excitement being a very large, very dead fish that got caught in my wake and stayed with me for a while. On the approach to Whittlesey there is a field where the acres have been turned over to an array of solar panels. It was a grey windy day when I went past these a couple of months ago and I looked at these solar panels sitting damply in the field and looked at the blades of the wind turbines turning energetically in the brisk wind and thought, 'I bet that farmer wished he'd invested in wind.' Today I looked at the gleaming panels on one side and the wind turbines standing still in the humid air and thought, 'I bet that farmer wished he'd invested in solar.'

I tied up at the lock at Whittlesey and went into the boat to cool down and get a drink only to find that when I shot down for water earlier I'd left the tap running and I'd emptied the water tank. I always have drinking water in bottles but it did mean my first task in Peterborough would be to get water. I hoped the water point and sanitary station hadn't been vandalised yet again and were working properly.

I was foraging in my weed hatch trying to remove bucket loads of blanket weed from my prop when a scrap of black fluff shot over the weir at the side of the lock and got lodged between the boat and the bank. It was a tiny, noisy moorhen chick. It is always a wonder how something so small can make so much noise. I'd have thought when you are that tiny it would be best to keep quiet and avoid alerting predators to your presence. But there are many moorhens on the rivers and canals so I suppose that evolution has it worked out: if the chick is separated from the mother it calls as loudly as it can and mother looks for it. And mother moorhens may be small and vulnerable-looking themselves but they do protect their chicks. I've seen a small moorhen fly at the neck of a swan that was too near her chicks. Even more effective was a Great Crested Grebe that dived under water and came back under a swan stabbing it with its sharp beak. The swan fled downriver in a great flapping of wings and splashing of water without even waiting to see what had attacked it.

I scooped out the chick with my new fishing net and carried it, still peeping loudly, to the other side of the lock where I could see a moorhen and two other chicks. I put it in the water and it scooted away almost running on the water to be re-united with its family. In its enthusiasm it got too near the pull from the weir and it was only the last minute intervention of the mother that prevented it going over the top and down the side-stream again.

I had a time booked at Stanground Lock, about an hour away and couldn't put off going through the lock any longer. I couldn't find my Middle Level key so I had to climb the fence, then I found I had the wrong windlass with me so I had to climb back again to get the correct one. Keys, windlasses, security locks, design of lock operations are different on every river and waterway. On the Great Ouse the protocol is to leave open the gate you have just gone through, on the Nene the upstream pointing gates have to be closed and the guillotine gates left open, on most of the canal system both gates have to be closed. The instructions at this lock are to leave the downstream gates open. The last person out had not only left the upstream gates open but had also left the paddles up. I had to close the gates, drop the paddles and fill the lock before I could go in. On the canal system this can be annoying but on a hot afternoon at Ashline Lock it was a torment. Each of the four paddles (or penstocks as they call them here) need a thousand turns to open and the same amount to close. Sweating, and swearing at the last people through, I put the windlass in the mechanism and started to turn and turn and turn. Two fat ladies leant on the fence and, in silence, watched my exertions.

As I continued on my sticky, sweaty way I did think it would be good to go for a swim in the 1930's Lido which is near the river in Peterborough but by the time I'd passed through the Stanground Lock, stopped at the water point and then moored up it was getting too late. A text from my friend saying she was sitting having a drink on the riverside terrace of the Keys Theatre and had a glass of wine waiting for me was adequate compensation for missing a swim.

We then took the ten-minute walk into Peterborough. For over twenty years I lived twenty-five miles from

Peterborough and for a few months I worked there. I always associated the town with a grim rail link, ring roads and roundabouts, multi-storey car parks, shopping centres and interminable waits in the passport office but what a difference a bit of town planning mixed with a mellow summer evening can make. The saplings I remembered along the centre of Bridge Street had grown into trees providing shade to the market stalls, the ugly building in the centre of Cathedral Square had been demolished and the area paved in stone and water jets and seating put in its place. That evening we sat outside Carluccio's restaurant and ate pasta and drank cool wine. The water jets were quiet, no children running in and out of them, only patches of wet stone remained to signify their presence. The sun was sinking, leaving a warm glow on the walls and arches of the seventeenth century Guildhall and the church of St John the Baptist. A steady stream of people was heading through the gates into the peaceful precincts of the Cathedral. The feel was not of an industrial East Midlands town but of somewhere warm and foreign. I do wish we had more warm evenings like this, it could make our perceptions of many of our towns more favourable.

We set off the following day. Once passed the two large barges (one a Chinese restaurant and one a bar restaurant) and passed a few blocks of flats, parkland stretches down to the river. The only clue that you passing through a busy city is the number of dog-walkers and strollers among the pathways that weave in and out of the trees. We passed through the pretty Ferry Meadows and under the centre of the lovely three arched white stone Milton Ferry

Bridge. By the time we reached the attractive lock at Water Newton my travelling companion had got the hang of working the locks and could get off and operate the guillotine gate without spilling a drop of her wine. By the time we reached Yarwell Lock I was getting tired. This tiredness combined with a sharp turn out of the lock, a breeze from the east and the flow of the river towards the mill stream meant I made an inefficient exit and got the boat's bows stuck under a tree. It took a while before I could get back to pick up Irene. I shouted to her that I couldn't get back on the lock landing and she should stand in the field and jump on when the boat came somewhere near her. She said she had a bad knee and was in no hurry so she'd wait on the lock landing until I remembered how to handle my boat properly. I did get there eventually and at least I provided a bit of entertainment for the watching campers and caravaners of Yarwood Mill who were out for an evening stroll.

It was getting late and dusk was gathering by the time we tied up at Elton and we were hungry. The cattle in the field had grown since I was last there; then they were boisterous youngsters and now they were lethargic teenagers. We skirted our way around the edge of the field trying to avoid both them and their deposits but they didn't seem in the least bit interested in us. We stopped to look at the 18th century mill standing on the riverbank. Most of the mills on the Nene have been converted to other uses. At Yarwell the caravan site has developed around it; at nearby Warmington the mill is a kitchen show room; at Oundle a hotel and restaurant; other mills along the Nene have been converted for residential use. As far as I am aware only Elton remains in its original state. Peering through the cracks in the boarding around the doors we could see the old mill wheel and other bits of machinery that we couldn't identify but must be useful if you wanted to operate a water-mill.

We went up the pathway and across the village green to the Crown Inn, it was surprisingly quiet for a Friday night but they told us they couldn't serve us. We begged and grovelled a bit, and explained we were on a boat and hadn't any other form of transport and Irene had a bad knee. The barman was surprised we had arrived by boat as he didn't know there was a river nearby. He went to ask the chef if he could fit us in, but came back with a, 'No, we are full.' We pointed out that there were only half a dozen people eating. The barman told us the deep fat fryer had broken down, we said, 'That's okay we don't want anything fried anyway.' The barman was adamant the chef wouldn't serve us, there was a sudden outbreak of shouting from the kitchen and the barman looked embarrassed. It seemed we weren't going to get any food there. I knew there was another pub and a restaurant along the main road so I suggested that we try that.

'How far?' asked Irene, 'because my knee hurts.'

'It's about a ten-minute walk,' I told her optimistically.

We set off to walk, after five minutes she was groaning dramatically and clutching her knee. 'Can't we get a cab?' she asked. The consummate Londoner she expects black cabs always to be thick on the ground. I explained to her, patiently, that she was now in the middle of the

136

countryside where black cabs don't just drive past. The words were hardly out of my mouth when a black cab drew up alongside us and asked if we needed a ride anywhere. We took the cab to the Loch Fynne restaurant and even I had to admit it would have been much, much more than a ten-minute walk.

After we'd eaten a very satisfactory meal we rang for a cab to take us back to the boat and told the driver we needed to be near the river. 'What river?' he said, 'I didn't know there was a river near here.' We gave him directions to the gate that leads to the meadow where the track leads down to the river. He thought it odd that he was dropping people off at the edge of a field late at night. He helpfully put his headlights on full beam to light us on our way and as we walked across the field in their glare we could hear his laughter echoing into the night, amused at the spectacle of two women stumbling across a field towards a mythical river.

Three days later (our cruise was a leisurely one) I arrived back at my mooring at Barnwell. It was now September and I made the decision to spend another winter there. The river and weather had been too unpredictable this year to encourage me or even to allow me to venture further. I'd leave my sojourn on the canals for next year.

I was rather upset because for the second time in my short boating career I'd paid for a Gold Licence which I hadn't been able to fully utilise.

Part Four – Not Going Anywhere

Winter again

In December I was going through Corby heading towards Market Harborough to collect a book I'd ordered from a shop in the town. The road was closed because of flooding on the A47 and there was a diversion in place. I followed the diversion signs through Corby and up the steep hill to the village of Rockingham and at the top of the hill I stopped and I looked out over an inland lake, a lake that shouldn't have been there. It was flooded fields and there was water as far as the eye could see. There was no land just water. Stark black hedges were the only break in the grey sheen of wetness, marking the edges of these flooded fields. Random solitary trees emerged from the grey. A glimmer of sun-light broke through the dense grey clouds, illuminated a sliver of silver water and as quickly disappeared again. More rain was forecast and looking at the threatening sky it seemed to be imminent. I couldn't even see a road running through this recently formed inland sea so I turned around and went back home.

At Upper Barnwell Lock, a short distance downriver from my mooring, the water hurled over the gates forming a white, roaring torrent of a waterfall. At first the river swirled around the old mill building, that had been converted to a hotel and restaurant, then it got lazy and just went in through the rear kitchen door and out again through the main front entrance. There was always quite a crowd watching and commenting on the unusual sight of the river going through a building instead of round it.

Swans nests and dead sheep passed by the boat, at one point even a telegraph pole came by. The EA rang the manager of the moorings to warn them that the lock landing at Lilford had broken free and was heading our way. The moorers should have been worried that something of that size and weight was coming towards us; if it slammed into the boats it could cause serious damage. Their main reaction, however, was one of gleeful anticipation. The number of potential uses that they could put an escapee pontoon too was mind boggling and made me wonder how they had ever survived without one in the first place. But the pontoon never arrived, a few days later a scouting party went out looking for it and found it high and but not very dry in a field alongside the river. The EA were informed and eventually it was repatriated to Lilford.

This year I'd been indecisive (not an unusual state of mind for me) about my plans for the spring and summer and hadn't renewed the Gold Licence in December, if I renewed it in March I wouldn't get my prompt payment discount. Yet it was more than just the money that was making me think of staying put. I was moored in a lovely tranquil place and I hadn't seen it in the summer when the bank that rises above me is full of leaves and birds and flowers. There are summer events in Oundle that I'd never had chance to enjoy. There were friends and family nearby who could just come over for a day's cruising to some great pubs and through gentle scenery. This part of the River Nene either going up to Thrapston or down to Peterborough is a beautiful, bendy stretch of river. Even without going anywhere I could just sit on my bit of secluded riverbank and enjoy a BBQ or read my book. I might even get around to doing much needed repairs and titivations to Rea. My sister and I had planned a holiday around visiting her friends in Liverpool and mine in Scotland, going to the Edinburgh Festival and then coming back down the East Coast and catching up with friends and relatives in Hull. On an EA licence I could still (river levels permitting) go over to Cambridge, Ely and surrounding areas. Travelling around in a boat is quite time consuming and I think I wanted to just have some time to myself instead of spending an entire day not getting far.

My 'now plan' was to stay around the Nene and the Great Ouse for the rest of the year and then in the following spring I would become a continuous cruiser on the canal system. I'd do what I intended to do when I first bought the boat, that was to give up work, and do some proper travelling. I wanted to go North, visit York then to cross the Pennines and reach Liverpool, to do the Llangollen canal and the Pontcysylite Aqueduct and to really see something of the canal system. I wanted to travel on the River Avon and maybe this time reach the Kennet and Avon Canal and do the marathon task of the twenty-nine locks at Caen. But before that I intended to enjoy one last year around here where there are pretty places and friendly faces.

That was the plan and as I made the plan I conveniently forgot that so far my plans hadn't often gone to plan.

I forgo the Gold licence, bought an EA licence and relaxed. Although I hadn't got far the previous year I was constantly thinking about going somewhere. Not to think about planning a journey was as relaxing as not going on the journey itself. Not to be constantly looking at future weather forecasts and the river levels at gauging stations was relaxing. To know where I'd be at any time was relaxing. I could book work without wondering how I was going to get to the car from where the boat was moored because I needed to drive to some obscure industrial site in Hertfordshire or an isolated farm in Norfolk. My finances didn't allow me to turn any prospective work down just because I couldn't fathom out how I would get there if I was moored on an isolated towpath somewhere in Lincolnshire. When somebody asked me where I would be on a certain day, weeks ahead the answer would be, 'here,' instead of, 'it depends on the weather,' or even, 'I haven't a clue.'

I did wonder if my feet would start to itch when spring arrived but spring didn't arrive. There was a brief flurry of warm weather in March that gave the impression that spring was on its way then spring changed its mind. The end of March and the beginning of April were cold, wet and windy. Then we had snow. The sheep in the field above, waiting for their lambs to appear looked cold and miserable; fat grey lumps huddled together against the elements made greyer by the frozen snow adhering to their thick woolly coats. The daffodils that had been appearing were flattened under the snow. On the river the arrival of ducklings, goslings and cygnets had been put on hold. Like everybody else who had been longing for spring I wasn't best pleased with the weather but it did mean that any lust for boaty wandering was quenched.

It was the middle of April when I happily left the mud and frozen slush of the moorings to go to London for a week. It was the week of Margaret Thatcher's funeral and I was working in the City. Security was tight, streets closed, barriers everywhere and bus services disrupted. On the day of the funeral I worked in an office in Aldgate, fighting through the crowds to get there; then trying to concentrate on figures when every minute the boom of a canon being fired reverberated around the buildings.

A week later driving back to the boat through Cambridgeshire on a sunny, spring morning the bushes which had seemed black and lifeless when I left were now at last showing signs of coming to life. Bright green leaves were forming and white and pink blossom lined the branches. Freed from their constraints of grey snow the daffodils were standing up straight to meet the sun and in the fields above the moorings the Herdwick sheep had small lambs at their sides.

My feet began to itch but I'd made my decision and I wasn't going anywhere on the boat, well not going anywhere far away.

The Shed

In the winter moored against a river bank there are no passing boats to wave at, the canoeists and rowers have stayed snuggly at home, narrowboats and cruisers are tied up tightly in marinas and even the ducks have de-camped to calmer waters. When all sensible neighbours are staying indoors as much as possible it's the small things that keep me entertained. Yesterday, for entertainment, I was watching my neighbour build a shed.

Last week when a digger was on the premises, ostensibly to fill in the mammoth pot-holes that had appeared in the track, the neighbour had commandeered it for half an hour to dig out the foundations for his shed. We were all very pleased with this intervention because it meant that even more mud was spread around outside and really, honestly, we all like mud and we did feel that we could never have enough of it. It meant I could tramp even more dirt onto my boat and turn my white rug into a sludge coloured rug at a faster pace. Although what an idiot to choose to live on a boat and then buy a white rug.

144

Two days ago he prepared concrete to spread onto the foundations. As it was a windy day this had the added bonus of scattering white dust amongst the brown, caking mud and making my shoes, boots and rug a more interesting, variegated sludge colour.

Yesterday he set about constructing the shed. Although maybe it would be more accurate to use the words cobbling together rather than constructing for he was using the best parts of two sheds to make one shed. I could hear a lot of hammering and swearing and I looked out in time to see him standing back to admire the one wall in place just as it fell to the ground with a loud smash. He ripped up that wall and picked up another section from his pile of walls to replace it.

The next time I looked out progress had been made because the walls were up, although I wondered if there was a fault in the design because there didn't appear to be a door. I could hear him inside the four walls, still hammering, still swearing. I kept listening but I didn't hear any calls for help as he tried to get out so maybe there was a door somewhere.When I left my boat to go to the shops a door had appeared just where one expects a door to be. The construction was starting to look like a shed, not a thing of beauty, not even a well-made shed but it was definitely a shed. When I came back from the shops the shed had a roof. It was a rather precariously balanced roof but it was a roof.

Today the strong winds have blown the shed down and all that remains is a heap of splintered wood.

Maria

The Mechanical Magician had been asked to help deal with the sale of a boat. Sadly her elderly owner, Trevor, had had to go into care and his relatives were left with the task of disposing of the boat he had lived on happily for many years.

The Mechanical Magician had a potential buyer, a young lady, Maria, who wanted a boat to live on, had a mooring space arranged and just needed a suitable boat to put on it. The fact that this particular boat was old, the engine wasn't working and it needed a lot of TLC didn't faze her for she had been living in an old Mercedes van which took her around the country as she earned a living by busking. A long, elderly boat was an improvement on a short, elderly van. The boat was well built and well equipped the only thing lacking was an engine. That is a bit of a problem if you are planning on going anywhere but less of a problem if you have a mooring with an electrical supply and are planning on staying put. It can actually be an advantage to have a boat without an engine, as vessels with no means of propulsion don't have to pay the annual EA licence fees. To Maria what was more important than the mechanics was that the boat should have the right vibes, the right feel, the boat should welcome her on board and it should want her as its new owner. The first impressions were good, she could feel the presence of its original owner and his aura was benign. He was also a musician (she decided) so he was pleased to have her, another musician, on-board. She brought her mother along for a second visit and the impressions were still good. On a still, warm night she sat on the riverbank next to the boat, smoking, watching the sky darken and the moon rise. She was communing with the Gods as she sat next to the old, scarred, white boat. From the outside the aura remained favourable; boat and human were developing a mutual bond. She knew the Gods were telling her it was the right boat and she would be happy living on it. She decided to buy it. I'm a bit earthier about these matters and I'd always trust the opinion of a good boat surveyor over the opinion of the Gods, but in this case the Gods were right (and a lot cheaper than a boat survey) and Maria had acquired a good boat at a bargain price.

The relatives of Trevor emptied the boat and gave it a 'sort of' clean. Maria and her mother got the money together and they went to pay the Mechanical Magician the few thousand pounds required. They walked onto his boat with two Tesco carrier bags stuffed with used five, ten and twenty pound notes, many of them Scottish, many of them out of date. The Mechanical Magician and his wife blinked unbelievably at this heap of cash then they just got out the wine and all four of them spent a happy evening, talking, laughing and counting the money and putting it into piles.

The next step was to get the boat to its new mooring, as the engine wasn't working it wasn't going to get there by

147

itself so Bob was volunteered to tow the boat. I was commandeered to help. I was happy to help it was an excuse to go on a boat on a fine early autumn day when the hips, haws and elderberries where nestled in the darkening leaves of the bankside foliage on this loveliest stretch of river.

On a misty September morning I joined Bob and his boat to meet up with Maria and her Mum, Moira, to take the boat to its new home about four hours upriver. It was agreed we would have an early start, Bob would tow and I would work the locks and generally do as I was told. Maria and Moira were bringing breakfast.

Our departure was slightly delayed because Maria had to sprinkle tobacco across the bow of the boat and then meditate alongside her new home to ensure that we would have a peaceful and relaxing journey and that we would all live happily ever after. Then departure was delayed again because I had to be shown around the boat. It had been stripped of all the previous owner's belongings and was now a blank shell, an empty canvass, but I could see what attracted Maria to the boat. It had a good aura. Maria was planning on spending the journey doing some scrubbing and cleaning for although she was happy with the general aura of Trevor she was less happy with his more personal aromas and was determined to rid the boat of every last whiff of him.

Bob tied Maria's boat to the side of his boat and we eventually pulled away from the bank. If anything the mist had thickened as we moved off down the Nene. We couldn't see much beyond the banks where spectres of sheep, their legs hidden by the fog, appeared to float in the fields. Spikes of reeds loomed ahead of us then the bend of the river sent us away from their ghostly, beckoning arms. Yet it was bright and a pale orange sun was suspended in the misty, greyness of the sky. There was a promise that the morning would emerge from this chill mist into the perfect boating day. At Lilford there were curtains of spider's webs festooning the trees covering them in a wet, silvery sheen. The breaking sun hazily illuminated the fine filigree of the webs and turned the droplets of water to glistening diamonds. We glided slowly past, the beauty of the scene silencing our chatter.

Because of the early hour we hadn't expected to meet anybody but as we approached Lilford Lock the guillotine gate was closed and there was a boat in the lock. Bob hung back because if he'd moored at the lock landing the two boats strapped together would have obstructed the wide cruiser when it left the lock. We were also well back beyond the pushing and shoving of the flow from the weir that would have caused problems when he was trying to hold the boats still. We were close to the bank so there was plenty of room on the portside for the cruiser to pass but only a narrow channel on the starboard. On rivers and canals boats should pass starboard to starboard and this cruiser was determined to stick to the rules even though there was much more room on the other side and we were hardly in a busy shipping lane where passing on the wrong side could cause confusion to other boats. He squeezed past scrapping through the bankside bushes. 'You haven't left me much room,' he shouted bad temperedly at us. Maria smiled sweetly at him and as he passed she leaned over and sprinkled tobacco on the bow of

149

his boat. 'Relax, be happy, have a nice day,' she told him as the tobacco blew back into his face causing even more scowls and grumbles. If he'd had the chance to smoke the tobacco rather than inhaling he would have had a better chance of having a relaxing day.

The sun was breaking through the mist and there was now warmth in the air and Bob was making hopeful remarks about breakfast. The typical boating breakfast would have been at the least a bacon sandwich, if we were going for the full cholesterol, as Bob was hoping for, sausages mushrooms and eggs would have been thrown in as well. But Maria and Moira were vegetarian and not being seasoned boaters didn't know it was the law to have bacon aboard every boat. They'd brought along a big bag of peas in their pods, some lettuce and a loaf of wholemeal bread. Bob's face when he was passed a plate of lettuce sandwiches and a pile of pea pods was a picture. It changed from puzzlement to amazement then fell to an expression of utter misery. I thought he was about to cry like a baby because his long awaited and looked forward to breakfast didn't include one ounce of saturated fat. At that point I jumped ship and joined Maria and Moira on their boat, I couldn't bear the thought of the next few hours listening to Bob sobbing into his pea pods. It was at this point that he decided to tow the boat rather than tie it alongside, maybe because there were a few narrow bridges ahead or maybe because he could no longer bring himself to travel side by side with a bacon free boat.

After the trauma of a healthy breakfast the journey was gentle and uneventful at least it was for us on the boat

150

being towed. I was steering the boat. It always surprises me that a towed boat without any power still has any semblance of steering but it has and we carried on bump-free upriver. Maria abandoned the bleach and the marigolds and joined Moira and me at the stern. It was not the right time to be stuck in a boat scrubbing and cleaning; the day was too warm and sunny; the scenery was too tranquil and attractive; it was a day to be enjoyed. We started off having a pleasant conversation about busking and boating but then the conversation dumbed down and became girlie. Bacon-deprived Bob had all the work to do, when we got to a lock he drove in undid the towing rope and then pulled the towed boat in alongside, only to be joined by three giggling women. I climbed the ladder and operated the lock; sometimes Maria came with me and Moira went into the galley to make tea. She was impressed with Bob, she said unlike most men he didn't get flustered and just went about the tasks calmly and good naturedly. She handed him the cup of tea, asked if he'd like another lettuce sandwich and smiled seductively at him. The seductive effect was rather ruined by her having a bright green pea pod stuck between her teeth, although had it been bits of sausage Bob might have been interested. We reached our destination and parked the boat in its new home then Bob and I turned around and went back the way we came. My first task is to raid his fridge to look for some saturated fats to return his cholesterol to their normal high levels.

It was a great to be boating on a peaceful warm day with delightful travelling companions. It was three days later that there was a party in the clubhouse. The Mechanical

Magician had paid Bob for the diesel he had used and with the cash Bob had paid Bill some money he owed him. There was a bit of activity at the bar and the treasurer was called over. At the same time Bill was on the phone to his irate son. Evidently somebody had been passing out of date £5 notes and suspicious-looking Scottish £20 notes and Bill's son had been refused service in the pub because it was thought he was passing counterfeit currency. The money had passed from Maria to the Mechanical Magician, to Bob, to Bill and then onwards to Bill's son. The Mechanical Magician and Bob feigned surprise that anybody would have the audacity to try to pass out-of-date notes and strange Scottish currency then they quickly disappeared out the back for a smoke.

A Missing Door

It was a cold, damp November morning when I decided it was
time for the thermal-lined curtains to go up over the side-
hatch and the front doors. The front doors let in draughts and
the doors to the side hatch were of unlined steel. On a sunny
day, when they were closed, you could feel the heat radiating
from them. In the winter you could feel the patch of cold as
you passed along the corridor. With winter approaching I
didn't need draughts or patches of cold in the boat and I was
unlikely to be opening them to let in light and air for another
four months at least. I knew if the wind came strongly from
the west I'd have more than a draught coming through the
front door I'd have a howling gale. So, I put up the curtain
rails and fished the curtains out from under the bed where
they'd spent the summer. I fixed the long thick curtains over
the front door and a matching pair over the side hatch (they
may have been cheap, unattractive curtains but at least they
matched). I then decided there was a draught coming from the
top of the side hatch door and I'd somehow try to seal the
gap. I slung open the door, the hinge snapped and the door

fell onto the bank. I did wonder afterwards why I'd slung open the door with such gusto. I knew one of the hinges had snapped and needed repairing (I planned to do something about it soon) so it was to be expected that the second hinge would be vulnerable.

I looked to see where the door had gone; it had landed half in and half out of the water. As I looked at the door, looked at the bank to see if I would find it accessible to get down to retrieve the door then looked back at the door I was in time to see it slide slowly and elegantly into the water. Gradually it became fully submerged. At that point I wasn't concerned. I thought it would be against the bank where the water wasn't deep and it would be a relatively straightforward task to retrieve it. I went out and tried to reach it but even by lying flat on the bank I couldn't quite grasp it; all I got was a wet stomach. I went to search for my sea-searcher magnet; the hefty magnet that can bring submarines to the surface. I couldn't find it, then I remembered I'd lent it to somebody a few months ago but I couldn't remember who I'd lent it to.

I went along the line of boats accusing everybody of having my sea-searcher magnet but nobody admitted to being in possession of it. In the end Tony lent me his. I went back to the bank where the door had disappeared and started fishing. I could see the door. It wasn't far below the surface, leaning against the sloping muddy bank, and the magnet soon caught hold of it. I gently pulled the door to the surface but as it got almost near enough for me to grab it the door slid off the magnet and fell back into the river. I did the same procedure another couple of times with the same result although each time the door went deeper into the river.

I decided I needed help. I went to find Bill. We went through the same procedure, again the door came out halfway before it started to slide back into the river and before either Bill or I could manage to take a firm hold on it. He decided we needed some other implement to help us grasp the door. I knew somewhere I had a long metal bar with a hook on the end. I'd found it on the towpath and I didn't know what it was for but thought it might come in useful one day. Today was the day. I searched the engine room thoroughly for the bar with the hook on it but couldn't find it although I did find my sea-searcher magnet. Now we had two strong magnets and I got the boat hook from the roof; that should have made it possible to get the door completely out of the river. It wasn't. The door seemed to have developed a mind of its own and had started playing games with us. Just at the point of grabbing it, it slid off the magnets, evaded the boat hook and went straight into the river with a grand splash, each time moving further out and into deeper water. We decided on one more titanic effort, as soon as the thinnest edge of door appeared we'd both lean over and grab it, hold it very tight and pull it out. The door responded with its own titanic effort, evaded our grasp dived down into the river and disappeared under the boat. Back to the drawing board, or at the least back to the kitchen for hot drinks and a chance to warm up and get dry in front of the fire.

We decided that even though we couldn't see the door it still couldn't be deep under-water. On at least a dozen

155

occasions we'd almost got hold of it so with a bit extra planning we'd be sure to be able to get it out. We just needed some extra help so we commandeered Tony and as a bonus his dog, Molly, came too and stood on the bank and barked at us. Bill stood on the roof of the boat as a spotter and we let the bow of the boat drift out. When he saw the door laying on the riverbed he put the boat pole in to mark the spot and we tied the boat up with the bow sticking out. Tony and I leaned out of the side-hatch dangling the sea magnets; Bill perched on the gunwales with the boat hook ready to catch hold of the door. We located the door and gently, gently pulled it to the surface, when it was almost out of the water Bill leaned far over, bravely risking a cold dunking, to put the hook under the door. The boat hook took the weight of the door, we were almost in grasping distance when the boat hook snapped and the door hurtled back into the river.

One thing we did discover was that the riverbank shelved steeply and the river was much deeper than we had anticipated. The door had slid merrily down the mudslide of a bank and was now somewhere towards the centre of the river in deep water. This part of the Nene was beginning to resemble the Marianna trench of Northamptonshire. We went back inside for another cup of tea and to stoke the fire.

The tale of the missing door spread along the mooring. Three boys in a boat arrived and their dogs followed along the bank to join Molly in the game of barking at us. The first task was to locate the door; it was now invisible in the deep water. The boys moved along the river, one leaning over the edge of the boat wearing a snorkel mask, while the others held onto his legs. After about ten minutes they let out a whoop of joy. The door had been spotted. They offered to jump in the river and bring it up but we dissuaded them. It was hypothermia weather. The door was in the depths of the river out of reach of the sea magnets and boat poles so we needed a new strategy. We went inside for another cup of tea.

Alerted by the barking and general noise the Mechanical Magician arrived from one direction and the Landlord arrived from the other. It was decided that some special equipment was needed and they would be happy to design a new prototype device for getting steel doors out of deep rivers. After half an hour they brought said device back, it seemed to consist of lengths of wood and rope the two sea-searcher magnets and a grappling hook. I think the moorers here at Hills and Hollows are all graduates of the Heath Robinson School of Engineering. The Mechanical Magician and the Landlord got onto the roof with the 'door fishing' device. The boys brought the boat alongside and were instructed to act as spotters; Bill took his place on the gunwales. Tony stood in the boat and shouted at the dogs. I offered cups of tea to the door-fishers but they said complicated work like this needed something stronger and did I have any lager on board. And while I was in the kitchen a bacon sandwich wouldn't go amiss.

The fishers of doors caught the door. They walked it gently towards the bow and they started to raise it so that Tony and Bill could catch it; the door took one look at them and slid slowly off the magnets and into the water. They decided they needed another magnet and fetched a third one.

This one was a hefty beast and really did look as if it could raise submarines from great depths. They lowered it into the water and there was a moment of excitement when they thought they had caught the door but they had only caught the other magnets. They raised the tangled mess of magnets and found that they were indeed exceedingly strong; it took them an age to separate them.

The Magical Magician's two Jack Russel dogs joined the barkers on the bank. Alerted by the noise The Man Who Knows Everything drifted along, laughed said he could solve the problem immediately but wasn't going to get involved with a load of useless idiots, however, if there was lager and bacon sandwiches going he'd have some as well.

For the next hour, the door fishers fished, the boys in the boats got bored and started messing about and the dogs barked on. The Man Who Knows Everything continued to drink my lager while refusing to tell us the details of his simple solution to the problem. As the fog rolled up the river the rope on the prototype fishing device broke and they had to stop fishing for the door and go fishing for their magnets. Then it got dark and they all went home. Apart from the Man Who Knows Everything, he was ensconced in front of the fire finishing off my stock of lager. The door was still at the bottom of the river.

I had a frame with a Perspex inset which fitted the gap where the door should have been so I put that up, sealed it with tape and it kept the weather out. The door wintered at the bottom of the river.

It might have been well out of sight but it wasn't out of my mind, I made tentative enquiries about getting a new door made, I wondered if it was covered by my insurance but never got around to putting in a claim. I was in the bar one evening chatting to a man and told him about my door (well conversations in Boat Clubs are very limited). It turned out he was a PADI-registered scuba diver and instructor and ran training courses for divers. Retrieving a door from the bottom of the river was just the sort of practical task that would be ideal for diver training.

It was March when he and his trainee came down to the boat in full diving gear and jumped into the river. The water was murky and the only way I could trace their progress was by watching the bubbles floating to the surface. The bubbles went in progressively larger circles well away from the boat and the site of the door and into the centre of the river. The divers surfaced and re-established their bearings. The bubbles came nearer to the side of the boat and when they re-surfaced they were carrying the door. Yeah... celebrations all round.

After five months I was re-united with my door and I have to say that it didn't look any the worse for having wintered in deep muddy water. If anything it looked in better condition than its companion which had wintered in its rightful place on the outside of my boat. I cleaned and polished it and had it welded back on, removed the curtains and once more had a pair of poppies and a cold draught decorating the corridor.

Staying Put

So on my planned year of not moving did I manage to stay put? Almost. When the weather and river levels improved I did go for a short cruise on my now well-worn route across the Middle Levels, onto the Great Ouse and to Cambridge. I stayed around there for a few weeks, catching up with friends, visiting my son and his family and generally being open for any visitors who fancied a ride down the river.

When I was motionless on my riverside mooring I did take every opportunity to get onto a moving boat. If there was a cruise going upriver I was there. If a nervous new owner wanted companionship, I was standing at the stern giving bad advice. If a boat needed to be towed I was happy to help. If anybody wanted needed an extra hand on the seventeen locks of the Northampton Arm I volunteered.

Otherwise I did what I said I would. I worked and replenished the bank balance. I explored the area. Friends came over and we either went for boozy cruises to the Kings Head at Wadenhoe or The Falcon at Fotheringhay and we went for walks around the area.

160

I went for a holiday in Italy and in August my sister came over and we went visiting friends in Liverpool and Scotland, and we went to the Edinburgh Festival.

I had the added bonus of being nearby when my second grandson put in an appearance. He'd decided to enter the world rapidly, so when I got the call that he had been born I was ready to set off for the hospital. No need, I was told, they were still at home. He'd arrived a few minutes after the ambulance crew got there. He was just an hour old when I first met him; he was red-faced and looked extremely disgruntled at having been propelled into the world so rapidly.

Then, after all that, autumn arrived and all I had to do was to sit out another winter. That didn't seem to be so bad. I was going to stay in London in December, at my daughter's flat, when she and her boyfriend went back-packing through South America and in January I was meeting up with them to spend three weeks travelling in Ecuador. By the time I got back, the days would be starting to get longer and I could look forward, rather belatedly, to starting a life as a continuous cruiser.

Part Five – Moving On

On the Grand Union

After the physical work-out of stiff paddles and unyielding gates of the seventeen locks that is formerly known as the Northampton Arm once again I was back onto the Grand Union Canal. This time I turned left.

What a lot of people. What a lot of boats.

When I was moored on the Nene it was a busy day if six boats passed by, mostly there was only one or two. I, and most of the other river borne inhabitants, stood up peered out of the window and waved to the occasional passing boat. To these boaters passing by our linear moorings it must have looked like a row of meerkats popping up at the windows, then waving and smiling inanely to them as they went on by.

If I popped up at the window every time a boat went past on the Grand Union I'd be up and down like a tart's knickers, my right arm would have repetitive strain injury and my mouth would have set in a rictus grin. After the first one hundred or so boats had passed by, the novelty wore off and I sat firmly in my chair and didn't bother getting up to look out of the window and wave.

On my second morning on the canal a hazy sun was just breaking through overhead but it hadn't yet dispersed the mist which had settled on the water. The line of boats moored ahead of me appeared to be floating on air. Their multicolours softened by the gentle light, merged into a subdued rainbow stretching along the towpath and around the bend. From one or two of the boats, white smoke rose from chimneys and with the lack of wind fell around the roofs of the boats enhancing the misty fairytale appearance of the canal. It was a calm, mellow morning and the pale orb of the sun emerging from the mist above gave the promise of a glorious day ahead. It was going to be my perfect boating day; warm and sunny and with very little wind to send my rusty steering skills awry.

The day may have been gently coming awake but I was not, my brain was still in sleep mode and I'd still got the early morning grumps. I'm not at my best in the mornings. My crew member, Elaine, decided, rather than get her head bitten off every few minutes, she'd get off the boat and walk the mile or so to the first lock. I unhitched the boat, pushed off and Rea and I quietly ambled off down the canal after her.

As I passed a moored boat the side hatches were flung open and an angry man shouted, 'slow down past moored boats.' I mouthed an apology to him, after having been on the wide and deep Nene where there isn't the same need to reduce speed because moored boats aren't rocked around in deeper waters. I was just not used to the narrow, shallow canals where the wash created is much greater.

After I had apologised I looked at my instrument panel and saw that I was only slightly beyond tick-over and when I looked along the boat I saw I was creating very little bow wave and there was hardly any wash. I hadn't woken up enough to start opening the throttle and reaching the giddy heights of four miles an hour, I was still sauntering along.

I will re-iterate I'm not a morning person; I have a short fuse until I've been out of bed and consumed four cups of coffee. That morning it was still early for me and the caffeine hadn't hit in. I decided he'd over-reacted. I mentally rescinded my apology, turned around and shouted back at him, 'if you can't stand a bit of rocking go live in a f**g house.' He couldn't hear me because he'd closed the hatches but his wife was standing by the bow of their boat chatting to Elaine and she heard me.

She turned to look at me, amazed by the sudden invective from the water, while Elaine turned away from her and started walking quickly down the towpath, hoping to distance herself from this foul-mouthed woman of the waterways.

At the first lock another boat kindly waited in the lock for me to catch-up with them, so we could go through the next five locks of the Stoke Bruerne flight together. It was a glossy, well-polished boat, with gleaming brass-work, they were obviously fully paid-up members of the shiny boat brigade. The couple, and the requisite dog sitting at the helmsman feet, looked at me apprehensively as I approached the lock; obviously they were worried that I might do a bit of barging and scraping as I moved into the lock with them. It was probably the usual scenario of, 'never trust a woman driver.' I got into the lock neatly without touching their boat or the walls of the lock and feeling pleased with myself settled back for a chat with the other driver while the crew members did the hard work of closing the gates and filling the lock. The man at the helm was complaining about a boat with its front end moored on the lock landing. 'Couldn't you moor up to use the lock,' I asked him.

'Oh, no we had plenty of room but that's not the point, he shouldn't be there.'

I do think that many of the shiny boat brigade are in a permanent state of indignation. Maybe when I've been back on the Grand Union for a while I'll get into a similar frame of mind. I'll complain about the people overnighting at lock sides or at water points even if they aren't causing me any problems. I'll be moaning about people who leave lock gates open. I'll be irritated by over-stayers on short term moorings. I'll be wittering on about boaters who take too long working the locks and hold up other people. I'll get incandescent with rage if I can hear another boat running its engines after the

165

8pm deadline. If I feel the slightest bit of rocking as another boat passes I'll even be slinging my side-hatch open and yelling, 'Slow down past moored boats.'

At that moment, though, my morning grumpiness was fading and I was reverting to the relaxed mindset of a river dweller. No doubt this will change soon. Rea is a lovely boat and has the potential to join the shiny boat brigade if only her owner could be bothered to get out with the polish and Brasso. To get into the mindset of the shiny boat brigade I will have to compete with all the other polished boats on the cut and when I stop I'll jump out to swab the decks, wash the windows and remove every scrap of dust from the paintwork. Then with the reflections of the paint dazzling passers-by I will have the credentials to moan about other boater's habits; over-staying; mooring at water points; playing loud music and laughing until the early hours; tying their boats up incorrectly, leaving lock gates open; failing to close paddles and generally not behaving according to the rules of C&RT or the mores of the shiny boaters. I will join in the complaints about C&RT and the lack of dredging and maintenance of locks. I will be writing them letters of complaint when over-hanging trees have the audacity to scratch my perfect paintwork.

I will become the chief moaner of the waterways.

Downwards

After leaving the Stoke Bruerne locks behind, the boating was easy. The canal wends its way gently through open countryside. Yardley Gibbon sits above the canal, but we didn't deem it exciting enough to climb the hill to visit the church or the pub. We went under the ornate Solomon's Bridge and passed the flurry of buildings at Cosgrove, through the shallow lock and then it was onto the long curly stretch through and around Milton Keynes.

When you drive by car through Milton Keynes it is on an interminable ring road going around countless roundabouts. The city never seems to appear. Over grasslands, through trees there are glimpses of housing estates. There are industrial warehouses and office blocks but there is little evidence of the inhabitants of Milton Keynes, little evidence that these partially hidden houses contain people. I expected that, as the canal passed through Milton Keynes, it would be hemmed in by housing estates, populated by people. But it isn't, it is rather like the road system (without the roundabouts) in that the city never seems to impinge on the canal.

The area around Great Linford is delightful and my guide says that the village of Great Linford is magnificent. We contemplated stopping but didn't, magnificence will still be there when I pass by again. Milton Keynes is still somewhere to the right but we weren't aware of it. The 48-hour Campbell Park moorings are supposed to be the nearest to the city centre but I could see only parkland, there was no sign of a city. When I did stop to try and find a shop I climbed the steps to the top of a bridge and could only see roads and roundabouts. We stopped, again, close to where the map showed there is a shop. I could only see grass and trees but when I walked across the small parkland I found a parade of shops with their backs to the canal and surrounded by many houses. Somehow the town planners of Milton Keynes have done a good job of hiding the city from casual passers-by.

Cruising on: through the lock at Fenny Stratford where the drop is so slight that it makes one wonder why there is lock there. Maybe it was to give the boater a chance to stretch their legs. To add interest to a shallow lock they put a bridge across its centre. Then behind a wall they put a car so every time the bridge is almost opened the car appears needing to go across urgently and the bridge has to be closed again. That gives the steerer a chance to look over at the Red Lion pub and decide that it would be a good idea to visit it. We stopped at the pub for a drink.

Then onwards the weather was still warm, the clouds intermittent and the breeze light. Perfect boating weather.

168

Through the three locks at Soulbury where the gates on the last lock refused to stay shut. On the third attempt at leaving it closed we gave it up as a bad job; the canal should be busy at this time of year so another boat would be along soon. Then I got shouted at by a large, blonde lady moored against the towpath. As we moved off down the canal her voice, yelling about waste of water, inconsiderate boaters, people who don't know the rules of the canal, faded into the distance. If she was so concerned about an open lock gate she could have saved her breath shouting at me and tried to close it herself. She looked as if she needed the exercise.

In Leighton Buzzard the hire boats were three abreast alongside the canal leaving very little room to squeeze past. As canal law dictates on a day when hardly another boat has been seen as soon as an obstruction appears another boat is approaches from the opposite direction. It was a case of both boats moved forward towards the obstruction, then both stopped, then both moved back. The other helsman tooted his horn three times, this is a code for something but I couldn't remember what it is the code for. We both moved forward. Then I reversed so far back that it was obvious that he had the right of way. We both grinned as eventually we passed each other.

Unlike Milton Keynes, Leighton Buzzard does gather around the canal, we tied-up and wandered into the town. The market was closing for the day, which was a pity as it seemed a diverse and lively market. Leighton Buzzard has a pleasing town centre and after three days rural travelling we needed some urban buzz.

The next day I moored up near Startop's End for a change of crew, I'd miss Elaine, we'd had a good, happy journey. I waved her off and Bob and dog arrived.

We stayed at Startop's End for the day. In the canal large carp swam. Next to the 'No Fishing' sign a man and his boy fished. As the carp were obviously used to surfacing for food thrown to them by visitors it didn't look as if they would have much difficulty in catching one. 'If they catch one I bet they won't throw it back,' said Bob, 'they'll take it home to eat it.' Actually, he may have been right, listening to their voices they did sound Eastern European and to the Eastern Europeans catching a large, tasty carp and then returning it to the water is an anathema. It made me think that maybe roast carp was a good idea. I even looked up the recipe but this recommended leaving the carp in a bath of fresh water for at least five days to rid it of the taste of mud. If I kept a carp in my bath for five days, I would become attached to it. It would be a pet with a name and I wouldn't be able to slaughter it and eat it.

After Leighton Buzzard the locks began increasing in their frequency. At Marsworth Junction, where the Aylesbury Arm joins the Grand Union Canal there is a flight of seven locks leading down to Bulbourne Junction where the Wendover Arm joins. After the more isolated aspect of the canal, the invisible town of Milton Keynes and the buzz of Leighton Buzzard we were back into 'historic and attractive canal-land'. Back to picnic and barbeque areas. Back to old canal buildings now restored with other uses than that for which they were originally built. There is decorative ironworks factory in an old canal building and interesting examples of their work line the canal. Tring Reservoir, a nature reserve, hugs the west side of the canal and its paths are busy with walkers, its banks lined with fishermen.

I do like the busyness, the people, the ice-cream vans, the boat selling sweets. I especially like all the walkers on the towpath as now I have a man onboard we have reverted to the usual gender roles of the canals: man drives; woman does locks. With all these people about it meant I got a lot of help opening and closing stiff gates.

Up the flight of locks and onto the Tring Summit. It was a beautiful, warm sunny day. Sunlight filtered through the trees and dappled the water. The birds were in full throttle. The towpath was lined with fishermen competing in a fishing match. Bob slowed down as he approached the first fisherman and tried to move away from the towpath to avoid the long poles but the fisherman said, 'don't slow down, just drive at them, these poles are expensive they'll soon lift them.' We drove on and the fishermen lifted their poles and many waved and smiled at us. That was unusual for a fishing match on the canals, it must have been the beauty of the day, the sunshine that had cheered even the grumpiest of them. It was only as we passed the last participant of the match, tucked away behind a bridge, that we got shouted at. He was irate, maybe he hadn't caught any fish. 'All you f...! boats are coming through this bridge too fast,' he yelled. He didn't seem to take into account that the boats may have been coming through too fast because they couldn't see him; he was hidden behind the stanchions of the bridge. The beauty of the day must have had its effect on me as well because I just smiled and waved at him instead of responding with one of my usual, vitriolic comments.

Down to Cowroast Lock where a small stream filtered through chalk feeds the canal making the water run clear for a few hundred yards. Clear water on the canal system is an unusual sight. A boat had waited for us to join him in the lock. It was a single-handed young man with a large rottweiller on board. The young man was on the lock-side, the dog was at the helm making sure no-one stepped on his boat. My turn to drive. I drew in alongside him, we eye-balled each other. Only one of us was intimidated. 'Don't worry,' his owner shouted down at me, 'he's as gentle as a kitten.' A kittens one aim in life is perfecting biting and clawing so that as an adult they can disembowel small animals. I hoped this large dog was not planning on practicing disemboweling larger animals.

Our travelling companion stopped at the next lock and at the following lock we had to wait for a pair of Fellows and Clayton working boats to come up. As their engines put-putted rhythmically an immaculately dressed Charlie Chapin look-a-like took photographs. Was he travelling with the boats? A man dressed as Charlie Chaplin crewing a pair of historic boats was incongruous. Historic boat crews dressed as old bargees, with red neck ties and carrying oily rags, they are definitely not dressed in suits, spats and carrying canes.

Into Berkhamsted where the locks were arriving thick and fast and the canal side pubs were spewing customers across the towpath. At the Rising Sun Lock a group of customers picked themselves up from the grass outside the pub and came to peer in the windows of the boat, speaking to neither Bob, the helmsman, or to me, the lock operator, just commenting amongst themselves about the interior. I knew I should have made the beds.

After another two locks we stopped for the night where the towpath bordered gardens. It might have been a bit more peaceful further on but the next lock was called Sewer Lock and that didn't sound a very fragrant place to moor. Here there were no noxious smells. There was only the smell of mown lawns and barbeques. The children playing cricket were starting to sound fractious. It was the end of a long, hot weekend and it seemed that there would be tears before bedtime. The sounds of the arguments were regularly drowned by the screech of the Virgin Trains on the other side of the canal. The knowledge that school and work loomed the next day must have been fraying tempers. Not for us though, ahead of us was another day of ambling down an attractive canal without a care in the world.

The following day we pulled up at Winkwell to operate the bridge. The Three Horseshoes at the side of the canal looked tempting but it was too early in the day to stop. The road bridge over the canal had to be opened to allow the boat through. Although the road appeared to be a quiet country lane there was a steady flow of vans and cars from each direction. I waited until the road was clear, inserted the key in the lock pressed the button and red lights flashed and the bridge slowly opened. Cars arriving from both directions stopped and Bob brought the boat through the open gateway. What a wonderful feeling of power I got from stopping the traffic. I re-opened the bridge to traffic, acknowledged the six cars and a van that I'd delayed and went back to the boat.

The power of stopping the traffic had obviously gone to my head because three hours later when we stopped for water I couldn't find my keys and realised that I must have left them in the gate mechanism at Winkwell. It was too far to go back to see if they were still there. My door keys were on the ring but I had spares, there were two other keys but I never worked out what they were for so they were no loss, the only one that needed replacing was the BW key that opens water points, sanitary stations and security locks. I stopped at the next marina and, reluctantly, spent nine pounds on a new key.

Onwards and downwards. The locks were frequent and irritatingly spaced so that there was hardly enough time to make a cup of coffee and drink it before we had to stop for the next lock. We were within hitting distance of London but, again, urban sprawl does not seem to reach the canal, in fact it is the lakes and reservoirs, birds and vegetation that seem the main feature of this stretch of canal as it heads towards London. Then past Uxbridge the nearness of stations and habitation meant long lines of moored boats and our progress slowed down to a crawl.

Into London

Onwards; more miles; fewer locks. I overshot the entrance to the Paddington Arm because the signpost is obscured by a bush, then I had to reverse back and turn into the narrow entrance. Somehow, I'd expected the main canal route into London to be better signposted and the entrance to be more impressive but the start of The Paddington Arm is only impressive in a negative sense. It had an air of dinginess and an aura of neglect. It is industrial, litter strewn and unappealing.

Between Cowley Lock where we'd stopped last night and the flight of three locks at Camden this stretch of the Grand Union is lock free for 28 miles. Ahhhh that is my idea of boating bliss; twenty-eight miles of lock-free canal, no mooring up, no heavy gates, no wielding of windlasses: lovely. But this part of the passage, through unappetising warehouses and bleak car parks, while trying to avoid the debris in the water, is far from lovely. This section of the canal conjures up images of films of the 50's and 60's when the shot of youths gathered under a bridge smoking meant they were 'Up to No Good!' or a shot of a man walking a dog meant he was about to discover a body floating in the water. After the decline of commercial canal traffic and thereby the decline of the canals themselves much work has gone into restoring them. Since the nationalisation of the canal network in 1947 canal societies have worked tirelessly to re-open derelict canals, restore locks and old canal buildings and generally make the canals attractive to a variety of users. During the trip on the Grand Union, from Braunston, through Stoke Bruerne and Bulbourne I had seen how the care of the canal system and the restoration of its buildings has attracted visitors. I don't think there is much scope for the prettification of this part of the Paddington Arm, although a clear-up of the litter and debris in and around the canal would be some improvement.

We stopped for a lunch break, tying up using some convenient rings set in the concrete of the bank that we assumed were there for boaters visiting the pub alongside the canal. We, somehow, failed to notice the large tap and prominent notices asking boaters not to moor here unless they are taking on water. The people on the boat who did want to stop for water told us in no uncertain terms that this is a water point and we shouldn't be moored there but they curtailed their lecture when the look of surprise on our faces when the notices were pointed out to us proved our crime was not intentional. They drew up alongside and threaded their hose across the roof of Rea and we all talked the usual canal talk, about where we're heading and where we've been, while their tank filled. Our conversation must have been more interesting than I'd imagined because, water tank filled, they then said

176

good-bye and headed off in the direction of Bulls Bridge without detaching their hose from the tap. The hose swept across my roof removing plants and planks then got caught in my bike. The end that was still attached to their boat fell with a splash into the canal. We all sprang into action to rescue the hose, detached it from the water point and untangled it from all the cack on my roof. I supposed the upturned and broken pots of herbs were my comeuppance for committing the heinous crime of mooring at a water point.

We started to move off from the bank but the passage was blocked by a wide-beamed boat ahead of us, it was a trip boat dedicated to teaching school children. Twenty multi-hued children in blue sweatshirts leant over the bow and listened to a teacher giving a talk about the wildlife of the area. I'm not sure what he could find to talk about in this murky semi-industrial stretch of the canal where much of the usual watery wildlife is conspicuous by its absence, maybe he would be better improvising about what can be seen colonising the water and towpath.

'Look to the left and you will see a swarm of white plastic bags, these have the distinctive blue and red markings of their breed, further on we will find another breed of plastic bags that are bright orange. Oh, quickly look to the right where we can see the colourful plumage of a KFC carton. Just ahead of us are a flock of polystyrene cups, these are a hardy breed of drinking vessel and will live for many, many years. Keep an eye out for the many types of can floating in the canals and along the bank-side, all have their own markings. If you see a glitter of gold under the benches that will be a

177

Special Brew can, they are prolific breeders along the towpath where they like to congregate around benches. If you could see into the water you would be able to see that hardy canal animal the supermarket trolley; they are sometimes found in the company of the bicycle wheel. Sadly, it is often difficult to spot them because the water is so polluted we can only see the top few inches of anything. Watch this narrowboat passing by they usually manage to pick up interesting floating objects on their propellers, oh yes, it is stopping. Please put your fingers in your ears children because the language that boaters use when they pick up plastic bags on their props isn't suitable listening for ten-year olds.'

Whatever the teacher was saying was fascinating to the children, they moved, in a pack, from one side of the boat to the other. We watched their group movement rocking the boat as we followed its slow progress back towards its base in central London.

Although the canal may be devoid of wildlife it has a wide variety of smells. Not just the nasty smell of sewage or decay emanating from the canal but the delicious smell of cooking from the bank. At Northolt there was the smell of bacon frying. From the café at Alperton the smell of a turkey roasting brought a sudden remembrance of Christmases spent with my parents. Mostly the smells come from the premises in the industrial parks along the edge of the canal. Baking bread was replaced by the smell of curry, followed by scent of vanilla for biscuits. A tray load of fragrant samosas was being loaded into the back of a refrigerated van. Meat pies were being made in a factory to our left and the scent of onions frying and beef braising made us feel hungry.

Trying to find a desirable mooring along here was trying. The area around Perivale, opposite a golf course and open parkland, was pleasant but the potential moorings were already taken. When we tried to moor at the end of the line of boats we ran aground on mud and the boat was too far away from the bank to even allow the gangplank to be put down. Eventually we plodded on and stopped for the night opposite Kensal Green Cemetery, hoping it would be peaceful. The residents of the cemetery wouldn't be making too much noise and the gasometer on the towpath side looked well-behaved. The night was cloudy and moonless but we were in London and the ambient light from beyond the railway cuttings and marshalling yards to our right reflected a dull orange glow onto the low cloud. It gave me enough light to see by, even without a torch, when after a visit to the supermarket, I walked back to the boat along the unlit towpath.

The dead and the gasometer may have been quiet but the goods trains heading into Paddington were not. Their speciality was an ear-piercing, teeth-on-edge screeching of brakes which reached a crescendo in the early hours of the morning. The next day, at the crack of dawn, the pile drivers, working on Cross Rail, started pounding and if I'd intended to have a lie-in it would not have been possible. I had a few days' work booked in London and Bob was heading back to his boat so, despite the noise from the building work and all the cyclists speeding along the towpath and all the trains screeching, I decided to stay there for the seven days that is

179

the official, allowed mooring time. The following evening, I came back to the boat after working in the City to find that Rea was not where I had left her. She'd made an escape bid. I spotted her a couple of boats away. It was obvious that the mooring pins had been pulled out of the bank and she had headed back down the canal. Somebody had kindly retrieved her and moored her up once again. I took the precaution of hammering in two extra sets of pins as the bank was soft and there was constant waterway traffic. It may have been a speeding boat that had dislodged her but more likely it was one of the many passing wide-beam boats. These are between ten and twelve-feet wide and this extra width does mean that on shallow canals they drag a lot of water. Even when passing at tick-over they cause moored boats to pull at their pins.

In the duration of my stay here I was able to return my unknown saviour's efforts by helping retrieve and re-pin two other boats that had been dragged off their moorings and were floating away with their ropes dragging in the canal, pins still attached.

Normal People

The Canal and River Trust chuggers are out in force on the towpath outside the Sainsbury at Kensal Rise. They're next to the overflowing rubbish bins where rats dive in and out looking for titbits. They have their leaflets and other paraphernalia on the bench where the wino's usually congregate. They're trying to stop the cyclists that are speeding past and the walkers hurrying to work so they can extol the virtues of C&RT and to get them to sign up to make contributions towards the expenses of the Trust. They aren't having a lot of luck in getting, otherwise preoccupied people, interested in donating to the charity.

I'm mooring up to visit the supermarket and as such I am relatively static and an easier target for the pretty young girl's sales spiel than the cyclists and the hurrying workers. Although, she doesn't take into account that a lone woman trying to pull in sixteen ton of steel against a strong breeze is hardly likely to drop everything so she can sign up for a monthly direct debit. She rabbits on about the environment and the wildlife. After a lot of heaving and pulling I manage to successfully tie the centre rope and then go to the front of the boat to get the bow rope, she follows me yattering about the number of people who use the towpaths for recreation and stresses the health benefits to all the walkers and joggers. I head back towards the stern and she follows me, again telling me about the historical aspects of the canals and the canal system and how the canals are part of the industrial heritage of the country. As I'm closing the stern doors she reaches the end of her set text.

'Would you be prepared to contribute towards the charity?' she asks.

'I already do, I give a £1,000 a year,' I tell her.

'Oh, that's very generous is it a voluntary contribution?'

'No, it's my licence fee for having a boat on the canals.'

She looks perplexed, 'I don't really know anything about how it works with boats on the canal.'

'Doesn't your training include details of the boats and boaters and the licence fees they pay?' I ask her.

She shakes her head in puzzlement. 'No. People on boats aren't mentioned in our training,' she says, 'we're only taught how to approach normal people.'

Paddington Basin

I moored in Paddington Basin. By the skin of my teeth I squeezed into the last available mooring alongside a wide-beam boat. The yellow jacketed security guard watched me try to steer in, shaking his head dubiously at my attempt to get both me and the boat to breathe in and manoeuvre into the narrow space. When I eventually did slot the boat into the space he grinned and gave me two thumbs up.

Do I like the seven-day moorings in Paddington Basin? I'm not sure. They are certainly convenient for the centre of London; they are safe with security guards patrolling this area of brand-new high-rise offices and flats for 24 hours a day. The developers have put thought into the landscaping of the area with fountains, statues and one bridge that curls up and another one that opens like scissors. The full development of the area is not complete and when it is finished and matured and the high-rise cranes have disappeared and the constant noise of building work has gone it should be a good urban area to work or live in. Will it a good place to moor a boat for more than a few days? I'm still not sure.

My sister has joined me for a long weekend. My daughter and her boyfriend are back from South America and are having a party to celebrate their return and to celebrate their engagement. Marcelle has no doubts about the mooring at Paddington Basin. She does not like it. She dislikes being surrounded by high rise buildings, by the constant noise of footfall, of the rumble of cases trundling over cobbles, of conversations only feet from where she is trying to sleep, of the clatter and bangs of building work. She dislikes the constant drone of the generator at St Mary's hospital and the lights on the buildings and the walkways that stay on all night. She dislikes the volume of people and to cap it all she says the man in the boat next to us pees over the side.

I get defensive about my mooring and point out that for pure convenience and safety Paddington Basin is unbeatable. Where else could she get free accommodation smack in the centre of London? Anyway, the man next door, a friendly Geordie, is not peeing over the side of his boat it is his shower and sink outlets that are pouring water into the basin if he had a bladder large enough to accommodate that volume of water he would be in the Guinness Book of Records. In truth, although I have no visual evidence to prove it, he probably is peeing over the side. The sanitary stations in London are few and far between, the pump-out facilities are expensive and if you have to move the boat to access a sanitary station then you are liable to lose your mooring. If I'd been born with the necessary equipment, I'd pee over the side as well.

The morning after Marcelle arrives I take two bags of rubbish and our empty wine bottles to the disposal unit at Little Venice. It's about a ten-minute walk across bridges, passed pavement cafes, passed the entrance to the underground station where I have to plough through a bunch of Italian students. It isn't until I reach the facility that I remember that I need a key to unlock the gate.

There is a boat pulled up at the water point and I start to approach him to ask if I can borrow his BW key but his phone rings and he answers it. Rather than wait for him to complete his call I go along to the young man on the boat behind which is waiting for the water point to be free and ask him if I can borrow his key. He says, 'OK' and pops down into the boat to get a set, comes back and hands them to me.

I make my way to the gate and then look down at the set of keys he has handed me, at the grubby rubber underground motif of the key ring and stop in amazement.

'Those are my keys,' I tell him.

'Really,' he said, 'I found them in the mechanism of the swing bridge at Winkwell. I've posted notices on the London Boaters and other Boaters forums.'

Of all the boats in all the canals I have come to the right spot at the right time and purely by chance have found the person that has retrieved my keys from a bridge twenty miles away and over two weeks ago. Call it coincidence, call it serendipity, call it what you like but I think it's just plain creepy.

A Tourist Boat

In Paddington Basin there is a maximum of seven days' mooring and a man on a bike comes around each morning to check boats to determine their length of stay. It is not worth trying to bend the rules. I moved away when my time was up. The water point was empty when I moved off so I took advantage of that rare occurrence and filled the tank. As I moved away, two Japanese tourists ran after me waving tickets in the air, obviously thinking that I was the trip boat going without them. I was tempted to turn back, pick them up and charge them £20 each for the trip down to Camden Lock and back.

After a week in Central London I actually started to feel like a trip boat, one of the big boats that start from Little Venice and then make their way along Maida Vale, through the Maida tunnel, through St John's Wood passed Regents Park and the aviaries of Regents Park Zoo and then do a sharp left-hand turn towards Camden Lock. Then they leave their passengers to enjoy the doubtful and crowded pleasures of Camden Lock Market and pick up a new batch of tourists to return to Little Venice.

My daughter and her friends, a friend and her daughter made the most of me being in London and came for free boozy cruises along the same stretch of water for which they could be paying a small fortune on the official trip boats. I was soon on nodding terms with the trip boats, the cocktail cruise boat and the punt with the guitar playing singer sitting in the bow entertaining the guests. They're all friendly and smiley, unlike the man driving the boat that's equipped for group educational tours who hurled abuse at me for having the audacity to continue my traverse through Maida Tunnel instead of reversing and letting him through. I passed by him on a couple more occasions when I was in the vicinity, heard his surly and bad-tempered comments and concluded that he must be the rudest man on the waterways.

By following the trip boats or passing them on the canal I overhear so many snippets of commentary that I could do my own tour. On passing the length of residential boats in Maida Vale '....and here is where Richard Branson used to moor,' then further on the commentary starts again '...the MCC cricket ground was here before it moved to Lord's,' and then 'this is the house of the American Ambassador (to be fair I'm unsure which of the opulent detached houses is the American Ambassadors so I just wave my hand around a bit as we pass by this corner of Regents Park.) Then I can point out the aviaries designed by Lord Snowden and we can all peer into them to try and see birds of interest. On the south bank of the canal the much more interesting and accessible wart hogs watch the back of our heads as we pass on by. I start to feel that the other tour operators will soon insist I get a licence to ply my trade.

By the time my third batch of visitors arrived I had moved out of Paddington Basin and I was moored at Little Venice. In Little Venice I felt even more part of the tourist trade of London. In Paddington Basin the passing population were mainly workers in the offices. In Little Venice, although only around the corner from Paddington, it's more the leisurely and touristy. Bikers are banned (supposedly) from this section of towpath and although the moorings are alongside a road it is comparatively quiet for the centre of London. I'd moored against another boat at first but the charming young couple who had helped me pull in and tie up had left after a couple of days and I had taken their place against the towpath: a towpath busy with walkers, joggers and tourists. The boats moored alongside the towpath are frequently photographed, peered into and even climbed over by visitors wanting a better look at this colourful part of the canal life of London. My neighbours told the tale of sitting on the roof of their boat one evening, relaxing after work when two Japanese tourists walked on the boat, ignored them completely and proceeded to stand by the open door taking photographs of the interior. That was a bit excessive but in general if you don't want people peering in the window, photographing the boat or you object to having personal questions asked ('Why do you live on a boat? How much did the boat cost? What do you do with the sewage?') every time you step out then don't moor in Little Venice. Personally, I rather like it. I think being part of the tourist trail has unleashed my inner exhibitionism. I'm happy to have my boat photographed. I'm happy to chat to unknown foreigners and if they are particularly admiring of the boat I'll even invite them in to have a look around. The added bonus is, because people are continuously peering in at the window or asking to come onboard, I make sure the bed is made, there isn't any washing up piling up in the sink, the carpets are brushed and the boat is tidy. Living on a tidy boat makes a pleasant change for me.

When Irene and her family arrived and settled down on board it was good to see them but I did rather hope they would say they didn't have time to cruise the Regents Canal. I was happy to amble along the Regents Canal, yet again, but rather reluctant to vacate the mooring at Little Venice because I knew that the minute I left somebody would sneak into it and I could be searching for an age for another place to tie up. Unfortuantely they seemed keen to cruise.

I was pointing in the wrong direction for the cruise to Camden Lock, if it hadn't been so busy on the canal I would have reversed back and then turned. But it was a breezy, sunny Sunday morning and boats were waiting three abreast at the sanitary station and water point and there was a constant flow of traffic along the canal. I didn't trust my reversing skills amongst all those boats and with that wind blowing. I set off for the nearest turning point, about two miles away at Kensal Rise. There isn't anywhere else to turn a sixty-foot boat on this stretch of canal, I'd watched a boat turn under the next bridge but it seemed a tight fit and I didn't want to risk getting stuck. As it was I chose to turn at a point that had an inlet but wasn't the official turning point and

189

nearly got stuck anyway. It was an hour later when I returned to the point at Little Venice where I been moored and sure enough my space had been filled and another boat was just tying up alongside that one.

Once the novelty of getting her three-year old granddaughter to shout 'echo, echo' through the Maida Tunnel had passed Irene decided she was hungry and we should moor up for lunch. I knew from my many trips along here that there is nowhere to moor until just before Camden Lock. She was sure that I just hadn't been trying hard enough to stop. She started to look for a stopping place.

'You could put it on that sticky out bit between those two boats,' she decided

'That's a finger pontoon and they're private moorings.'

'Well there's a space. I'm sure they wouldn't mind.'

'Would you mind if somebody parked on your drive to have a picnic?'

'Probably.'

We travelled a few hundred yards more.

'There's plenty of space here and there's a pretty view of Regents Park.'

'It's solid concrete with nowhere to hammer the mooring pins in. If you fancy standing on the bank holding the rope for an hour, we'll stop here and I'll pass a glass of wine and some bread and cheese out to you.'

We went a bit further, waving to the tourists on the tour boats as we passed.

'There's a nice grassy bit here we could get out.'

'It's the American Ambassador's residence, we'd probably all be shot before the first pin was hammered in.'

We went another couple of hundred yards.

'There's a nice jetty there and it's got hoops to tie up on.'

'It's the stopping place for the trip boats to drop off their passengers at Regents Zoo.'

At the seven-day moorings at Camden she spotted a place, I'd got so used to disagreeing with her that I automatically said, 'It's too small.' But as I passed it I thought I might just be able to fit in. It was an odd space with a piece cut out with steps leading into the canal and would have been difficult for me to moor by myself because I would have stepped from the stern into the water. However, I had crew. I turned before the locks, came back and told Irene to get off at the front with the rope. Because of boats in front and behind and the cut-out in the towpath she had to leap off the boat. She managed it without breaking any bones or getting a dunking and I squeezed into the space with an inch to spare at bow and stern. Then the engine wouldn't stop. I punched a few buttons, turned keys and lifted the lid to the engine compartment but the engine still chuntered on merrily. When it comes to anything mechanical I am well aware of my limitations, so I went to the next boat and asked a kind looking man lunching there if he could help. He came back to my boat but he hadn't got much more idea than I had. He said he had a mate on board who is a mechanic but the said mate said it was his day off and he wasn't interested in looking at engines today. At the third time of asking the mate strolled over, glass of beer in hand, sighed heavily, leant into the engine compartment tweaked something and the engine stopped. He stood up took another swig of his beer, of which he hadn't spilt a drop, and went on his way before I could ask him what he had done to stop the engine. If it happened again I still wouldn't know what to do.

Now I was moored there I decided to stay, I had a couple of days' work in the Cambridge area the following week so a stay on a seven-day mooring would be convenient. I was sure my guests could find their own way home from here, they didn't need taking back to their cars in Maida Vale.

I woke the next morning to the sound of herring gulls mewing overhead. I looked out of the window and saw a black and white cow standing on the balcony opposite, for a while I was disorientated and didn't know where I was. Then a train trundled past on the bridge that crosses the canal and behind me children gathering in the playground of the school sounded like schoolchildren the world over. The towpath gradually became dense with cyclists and walkers on their way to work. Ahh yes, I am in Camden.

The plaque on the wall says that the curious delve with steps to the towpath was created to enable the horses, that long ago pulled the boats, to climb out of the canal. Trains passing on the rail bridge frequently startled the horses into panicking and falling in the canal, the steps were for them to get out. Poor old horses they did have to work hard, but then so too did the bargees that worked with them.

I Want Your Bike

I'm moored at a few hundred yards from the bridge at the end of Harrow Road. It's the middle of the afternoon and I'm sat at my dining table using my computer, ostensibly working but actually playing spider solitaire, when there is a knock on the roof.

A well-dressed middle-aged lady is standing on the towpath outside the door.

'I want your bike,' she says.

I just give a puzzled frown.

'I need a bike,' she continues in a strong French accent, 'and yours will be perfect for my needs.'

'What do you need a bike for?' I ask her.

'I need to find work and to find work I need a bike.' I wondered if she still remembered the slightly misquoted advice from Norman Tebbitt to the unemployed of thirty years ago to 'get on their bikes to find work.'

There is a pause while I consider this request, or rather this demand, for my bike.

'… and you don't use it,' she adds accusingly.

'Yes I do,' I say indignantly, 'I use it regularly if I am moored in a remote spot I use it to get to the shops or I use it for exploring the countryside. I need my bike.'

We both turn our heads to look at the bike chained to the roof. That I use it regularly is quite obviously a palpable lie, the bike is rusty and a pile of leaves and dirt has gathered between the bike and the roof. In all honesty it is too heavy for me to lift off the roof and the one time I did use it I couldn't get used to the back-pedal brake and when I accidentally back pedaled the bike stopped abruptly and I fell off.

She looks back at me and whips off her sunglasses, one eye has a heavy white bandage on it and the visible surrounds look bruised. If she thinks she's going to get a sympathetic response because of her injury she's chosen the wrong person.

'I need a bike,' she repeats.

'Well you're not having mine,' I say firmly. I close the door and go back to my computer. I presume she heads off to another boat with a bike on the roof and demands that they give her that.

In retrospect I thought if I really had the soul of a writer I would have invited her in, given her a cup of tea and listened to the story of why a well-dressed French woman with a black eye was roaming the towpaths of London begging for a bike. It could have been a basis for a novel or at the least a prize-winning short story. Although however tragic her tale, however heart-rending her story I still wouldn't have given her my bike.

Travelling in London

Backwards and forwards across London for a couple of weeks: Kensal Rise to Paddington and all points between. I'm enjoying being in the city. Hot days, mild nights and London's population is spilling onto the pavements, music from open windows, a constant stream of people along the towpath. The atmosphere is convivial, boaters chatty and friendly sitting out in the bow after a day at work. Fake grass on roofs seems a popular feature of boats around here, so boat dwellers can relax on the lawn with a chilled glass of wine.

On a still evening the sounds travelled along the water. Across the canal on a bench sit three twenty-something blokes wearing shorts their legs stretched out if front of them discussing who has the hairiest legs. 'I think Andy's legs are hairier than mine.'

'Maybe but if Andy stands up you'll see his calves are bald.' Andy stands up and does a twizzle. 'Whereas both yours and mine are hairy all the way round.'

I got thrown off my mooring at Paddington Basin because there was going to be dragon boat racing. When I wandered past later another boat had taken my place and all the inside moorings were full again. That's not fair; why couldn't I have stayed put?

The dragon racing took place the following evening. It looked like a corporate event, lots of city types, in team t-shirts sipping champagne. I watched for a while but once the novelty of listening to the big drums reverberating around the high rises wore off it wasn't very exciting. Nobody fell in, no canoes sank, there was a long wait between races and I wasn't going to get a share of that champagne so I went back to my boat.

I had arranged to meet my daughter and her friend at Oxford Circus to visit the Photographer's Gallery in Ramillies Street. It is not a good idea to meet anybody at Oxford Circus without specifying which underground exit to meet at. It is an even worse idea to leave your mobile phone back on the boat. Eventually we found each other. The exhibition on the third floor had a parental guidance warning at the entrance. Clare decided that this meant it was not a suitable exhibition to take a parent to. It's embarrassing to look at rude pictures with a mother alongside, so she suggested I wait outside.

Moored at Little Venice again and a chance to observe the uniforms of sport: not the players, the spectators. In the evening stout red-faced men, wearing straw boaters and MCC ties, stagger from the direction of Lords towards Paddington Station. In the other direction white-shirted fans with red stripes on their faces stagger towards the pubs in readiness for the England World Cup Game. The common feature of both sets of fans seems to be that neither of them look as if they ever could or did play the games they are supporting and they all seem to need to imbibe a lot of alcohol to truly enjoy the matches.

I used to live in Maida Vale, in Warrington Crescent, not far from the canal. When I have the chance, I take my friends for a walk around the area, visit the pubs and bore them rigid with my reminiscences. I point out the flat I lived in, surprisingly it hasn't got a blue plaque outside. Even more surprisingly there is a pub around the corner from where I lived that I don't remember at all. I remember the launderette and I take a wash-load there just for old times sake (it costs twice as much as the launderette in Corby!). I remember the Warwick Castle and the beautiful, iconic Warrington Hotel but of the pub that was nearest my flat I have no recollection at all. I visited the Prince Albert to watch England lose a World Cup match. It's a Victorian pub with a well-established feel to it, not a 'I used to be a bank type of pub'. How did I spend three years only a few hundred yards from a pub and be unaware of its existence?

I make the most of my time in London, mainly by just strolling around. I visit a few galleries, go to Highgate Cemetery which is a wonderfully quiet oasis; a mixture of the tended and the unkempt. I visit the grave of Karl Marx, or at least his monument. I was surprised by some of the recent, famous residents of the cemetery, mainly because I didn't know they'd died.

I was moored against two short boats. In the morning a sixty-footer, a few boats in front of me, left so I decided to quickly grab the space before somebody else came along. I put my shoes on, started the engine, untied, set off and moored up deftly, then tied up securely while chatting to a few passers-by. Then I went inside and found I'd left the tap in the bath running (was planning on soaking a wine stained table-cloth). Full bath, wet carpets and empty water tank plus a drain on my newly charged batteries when I have to run the pump for an age to empty the bath.

I spent a night using only the water from my emergency bottles and the following morning moved over to the Little Venice waterpoint quite certain that I would lose my mooring space in the age it took the slow tap to fill my tank. I did. Almost immediately a tatty narrowboat, definitely a live-aboard, drove into the space. Just as my tank was full a boat moored against the towpath two boats back moved away and I slotted back into his much more desirable space.

Now I was moored against the towpath with a full water tank I had no excuse for not cleaning my extremely murky boat. Or maybe I should just move on.

Moving Through the City

Considering I'm in the centre of a very large city, it's quiet in Little Venice. In the early morning the first sounds are the thump, thump of joggers on the towpath. But I can't hang around this desirable part of London any longer; it's time to move away.

Bob has joined me for the journey through London to Limehouse and ultimately I'm heading up the rivers Lea and Stort. I move the boat to Kensal Rise to stock up the fridge, cupboards and wine rack at Sainsbury. It's best to have plenty of provisions on board as there may not be a chance to buy food on this journey through the most densely populated part of our country. On my way back through Little Venice the water point is empty so I stop to top up with water, that is more of an essential task than stocking the fridge because water points and sanitary stations are definitely in short supply on this busiest stretch of canal. We help a Black Prince hire boat pull alongside us. Its crew are seven ladies from Boston on a week's cruise through London. They're seven nervous ladies because they've never done this before and ahead are unknown locks and long tunnels. We impart words of wisdom and encouragement and then leave them to filling the tank, telling them we will probably meet up with them at the first set of locks. They are heading down to Limehouse Basin where a pilot is meeting them to take them up The Thames

At the first of Camden Locks many legs hang over the edge of the entrance to the lock and in the lock itself. If they were my legs and sixteen ton of steel was about to squash them against a wall I'd move. Some do but a party of Japanese teenagers stay where they are intent on their polystyrene containers of food. I come alongside, advise them to move but they don't look up from the noodles they are shovelling into their mouths. Is it the language barrier? Is it cultural? Is it their age and gender? I wonder if a group of British fourteen-year-old boys would concentrate totally on their lunch and avoid eye contact with a woman on a boat. I decide they too would probably risk the destruction of their lower limbs rather than be seen communicating with an elderly, female stranger. It's a boy thing.

The three locks at Camden are heavy. Bob drives and I struggle with the gates. At the second lock the group of teenagers arguing amongst themselves have a threatening air. I hold tightly onto my windlass and Bob locks the front doors. As I struggle to open the gate two of them break ranks and come to help me, showing a polite interest in the boat and asking pertinent questions about boat-life.

I wonder how the ladies from Boston will cope with crowds and heavy locks and nowhere to tie up because of moored boats. Our progress has been leisurely and we were

200

planning to go back to the first lock to help them but as yet they haven't appeared.

Then it's onto St Pancras and Kings Cross were the development is rife. Sometimes London seems to be one big building site. Cranes loom, buildings are under construction, old commercial warehouses are being renovated. There are no signs of recession here, London is booming. The area around King's Cross is especially busy with development. The old railway buildings are being renovated, St Martin's School of Art has taken over a disused nineteenth century granary store and overlooks Granary Square with its fountains and fake turfed steps leading down to the canal. When complete the area will combine old and new in what the planners say will be a 'vibrant development.' Even the steel casings of a gasometer have been preserved but will there be any room for boats to moor? And is the country going to tilt southwards because of all this frantic development? In the North of the country is all quiet and do building sites lay untouched?

Through Islington Tunnel we're hoping to find a space on the visitor moorings. Just outside the tunnel there is one space and we double berth against a shiny new boat inhabited by a shiny young man. He tells us, abruptly, that he is saving the space for a friend who will be along in a few hours. We say, 'tough we're here now.' He accepts the inevitable and changes into a friendlier mode and tells us we are in a quiet zone (confirmed by notices) where we can't run engines for more than an hour, we must keep noise to a minimum and not burn wood. 'Boris lives up there' he says pointing up towards a row of smart white houses, 'so I

201

suppose he makes the rules'. I can see Boris's point, who wants to pay a few million for a house in Islington and then be constantly reminded of the presence of the riff-raff living on the ditch beneath you.

Late at night there is the sound of a crowd singing and shouting. It gets louder as the mob approaches, I start to feel apprehensive about this approaching, rowdy gang. A narrowboat emerges from the tunnel with just three lads on the back singing their hearts out. The tunnel and the deep cut it emerges into have amplified the sound of three to sound like a crowd of one hundred. Boris won't like it.

The next day the early morning sound is that of bicycle bells mingling with the rhythmic thump, thump of the joggers. We set off towards Limehouse basin. It is a fascinating journey past new build housing, old warehouses, smart offices, derelict buildings and graffiti. Flotillas of children in canoes pass us, paddling furiously. Canary Wharf looms ahead. Lock gates are stiff and leaky. There seems to be a laissez-faire attitude from the boaters in these parts with boats double moored, sticking out, on lock landings and at water points. The gates on the downstream locks have all been left open. That wouldn't have been too bad but we must have been following either two boats or a wide-beam and that means I have to close the two downstream gates before I can empty the lock. Bob says, 'leave the gate open when we come out of the lock, everybody else seems to.' That behaviour just wouldn't do on the Grand Union Canal but then London is another country.

The rain starts to fall as we come to the end of the canal just before it reaches Limehouse Basin but at least we don't have any more locks to work. My map is wrong though and at the entrance to the Basin yet another lock hoves into sight. I am just about to let my boat out of the lock, when a boat travelling behind catches up. It is a member of the shiny boat brigade and he comes over and harangues me for leaving the gates open behind me. My excuses of 'Everybody does it here,' and 'I had to close two gates at every lock, you only had to close one,' are not deemed acceptable and I get an ear bashing about rules, regulations and conservation of water.

That evening, safely moored in Limehouse we venture out in the rain, not far, only to The Grapes pub, to stand on the balcony watching the river while trying to shelter from the downpour. An Anthony Gormley statue stands on a plinth watching the trip boats, ferries and police launches speed past. I have seen so many of the naked replicas of Anthony Gormley, in Cambridge, St Ives and Liverpool that I must know his body better than my own. The inhabitants of Liverpool seemed to have got fed-up of looking at his private parts as well because they had painted yellow underpants on some of the statues in Crosby.

The tour boats have been converted to Party Boats for the evening. Sometimes the beat of the music drifts across to us, at other times the wind takes the sound in the opposite direction and the dancers just gyrate to their own silent rhythm. The lights of Canary Wharf glitter to the left; downriver Tower Bridge looms; diffuse lights reflect on the water. Riverside London is very atmospheric in its veil of rain.

I wake the following morning to the sound of a church clock striking. I count the strikes to see if it's time to get up. Six, seven, eight, nine ….. surely not that late…… thirteen, fourteen…….. a pause ….. then it starts again one, two. There are obviously three unsynchronised church clocks chiming away in the vicinity.

I watch a narrowboat and a cruiser go out of Limehouse Lock and up along The Thames. The cruiser zooms off ahead, the narrowboat bobs after him. When he hits the wake left by one of the fast taxi boats he ploughs through the waves with his bow lifting high above the water, then disappears into a trough. He looks small and vulnerable against the wide expanse of the river. Do I want to do this later in the month? Of course I do. Really I do. All experienced crew welcome; bring your own lifejackets and Valium for me.

We leave the basin via the Limehouse Cut; we need to be near an underground station to get back into Central London for a theatrical experience. The moorings at Limehouse are only free for the first twenty-four hours and after that they cost twenty-five pounds per night. I love Limehouse with its mixture of boats: expensive yachts and towering cruisers, narrowboats and Dutch Barges. I love the wide expanse of the tidal Thames outside of the lock gates with the promise of sea journeys and foreign travel. I love the old warehouses and buildings intermingled with new developments along the riverside but I don't love it enough to pay twenty-five pounds for an extra night so I move on.

Limehouse Cut is packed with boats then interspersed with bleak stretches where nobody moors. If nobody moors there then there must be a reason so we won't moor there either. I was hoping to stop at Three Mills and look around the two old mills that are there (evidently one is the largest tidal mill in the world). The buildings and the area certainly look interesting and there is a space but I encounter the usual problem that a sixty-foot boat won't fit into a fifty-five-foot space. After ten minutes of trying to achieve the impossible I give up and move on. I'll stop for a proper look on the way back.

We move on past an endless variety of boats: smart, painted, graffitied, on the point of sinking. Large teeth painted on bows seem a popular addition to narrow-boats. Then move on past the entrance to the loop around the Olympic Park, which is still closed to navigation.

A C&RT weed cutter passes by, 'What's the mooring situation around here?' shouts Bob. 'Dire' they reply.

Just as we're about to accept that we will be travelling all day and getting a train in from somewhere in the depths of Hertfordshire, a boat ahead leaves and we pop into the vacated space. It turns out it is a very useful space, near to Hackney Wick station and a stone's throw from Stratford so the trip into Central London is easy. We go to the Rose Theatre: a strange, small theatre under huge girders that hold up the high rise above to protect the archaeological remains. It is an Elizabethan theatre which is still being excavated. It sells drinks but has no toilets (the toilets are in its sister theatre the Globe which is around the corner); this makes the second half of the performance rather uncomfortable. A friend of a friend is giving a one-woman performance alongside another one-woman performance. The theatre holds fifty but is only half full. Afterwards we all go to the local pub, cast and audience, and spend another evening standing, with drink in hand, watching the Thames glide by.

We are moored alongside the Olympic Park so the following day I take the opportunity to go for a swim in the Olympic Pool. It was easy to find the pool, it's wave-like roof is eye-catching but I did have a problem finding the door to get in. It's busy in the pool so I refrained from diving in from the podium and doing racing turns. I'll leave that for next time.

The flower beds around the stadiums are incredibly beautiful, masses of flowers; hollyhocks, red hot pokers and many kinds of wild flowers I should know the names of but don't. During the Olympics when these gardens were managed, and blooming in their full glory, it must have been impressive. It's a pity I didn't bring my camera. Next time I will.

Invasive Species

We're on the Lee canal heading towards Hertford. Bob is at the helm I'm in the galley making coffee. I hear a shout from the towpath.

'Hey mister will you give us a ride.'

'No.'

I join Bob at the stern wondering if he's being mean to little boys but when I see the towpath contingent I decide he's probably wise not to give them a ride. They are the stereotype of the sort of boys that boaters are warned about: the sort of boys that drop bricks from bridges or spit at boaters passing underneath or jump on roofs and run from one end of the boat to the other removing valuables as they go. They look like the same sort of boys who pelted me with maggots when I walked along the towpath earlier in the day. I might be being unfair to them by simply judging them by their appearance but it's best to err on the side of caution.

'Oh, why not mister, go on give us a ride our legs are killing us.'

'We've got a vicious dog on board, so you wouldn't be safe.'

The vicious dog sticks his sweet, shaggy head around the door and smiles at them. They burst into fits of theatrical laughter and bend over holding their sides shaking with supposed hilarity. 'That's not a vicious dog.'

'Don't you be deceived by his pretty face his mother is a Jack Russell and his father is a pit-bull terrier so he's a Natural Born Killer.'

The Natural Born Killer wags his tail and gives them a friendly woof.

They jog along the towpath keeping pace with us, aching legs forgotten. A bit further on and they have another request, 'can we borrow that stick with a hook on it, we've lost one of our nets and we want to fish it out.'

This time Bob relents, puts the boat in reverse and passes them the boat hook. They poke around in the water for a while and then bring up a crayfish pot, crammed with crayfish feeding on a large fish head. They untie the pot and then hurriedly leg it behind some bushes leaving the boat pole lying on the towpath. When we move towards the bank to retrieve the pole we can clearly see a line of crayfish pots in the water strung along the bank-side, all baited and crawling with crayfish. On the other side of the bushes there is a caravan site, with white vans parked outside the caravans and scrap metal piled high in the corner. We retrieve the boat pole and leave quickly. We don't want to be implicated in the crime of stealing crayfish and pots should the irate owner suddenly appear from the caravan site behind those bushes.

The pots were full of the American Signal Crayfish that are abundant on the River Lea. The much smaller British

Crayfish is a protected species, increasingly rare due to the thuggery of their larger more voracious American cousins and it was unlikely that they were in the pots. Yesterday Bob decided to fish from the boat I told him that I'd heard that cormorants had decimated stock on the River Lea and he wouldn't catch anything. In ten minutes he hadn't seen any fish but had caught five of these crayfish so put his rods away in disgust, and in an environmental unfriendly way he also threw the crayfish back into the river, a move which is frowned upon. A boat moored behind me put out a crayfish pot and within an hour had three crayfish in it. I was impressed. For years I'd been eating Pret a Manger's crayfish and avocado sandwiches, now I could be able to produce my own. I could see many a free meal of crayfish risotto, crayfish gumbo, crayfish in every known combination stretching ahead of me. I thought I would have a pot strung outside my boat as well, then I looked at the ugly creatures with that large black claw and knew I wouldn't have the stomach to handle them live and drop them into a pot of boiling water prior to peeling them.

Also, if I had put a pot out to catch them I would have been breaking the law and liable to a fine because a licence is needed to catch crayfish. Crayfish are proliferating in southern England and are a menace to fish and wildlife and their burrowing into river banks is reputed to make the banks unstable. Their hard outer shell means that they have few predators and they harbour a fungus which causes them no harm but that can kill the indigenous crayfish. I would have thought that as many people as possible would be encouraged to catch them and licencing would be counter-productive to the aim of ridding the waterways of these pests. But as I read on I could see the point of the Environment Agency wanting to licence crayfish catchers. A crayfish licence is free but there are restrictions as to where they are caught and on the method of catching them. The size and shape of the pots is restricted so that other wildlife isn't caught and harmed. They also wish to limit the number of catchers in any one area as they don't want crayfish wars breaking out on the banks of the River Lee. Obviously, there must be a trade in crayfish; they don't get into my crayfish and avocado sandwiches by themselves. The number of these pots strung along the banks of the River Lee would suggest a commercial operation, there is even an association for crayfish trappers (NICT) and these small crustaceans fetch a good price in the market place. Not as high a price as lobster, to whom they are related, but then they are not as tasty, their flesh is softer, sweeter and blander than that of a lobster. The wish of the EA and other environmental organisations would be to remove them completely from the waterways but evidently if all the crayfish catchers managed to catch a thousand a day it would have very little impact on the stocks. A thousand a day is an awful lot of crayfish risotto or crayfish gumbo, we all better start cooking. The meat of crayfish is fat free, full of omega-3, and vitamins A and D: a lot healthier than your average burger. Though if we want to help rid our waterways of crayfish then check the country of origin before buying, much of the crayfish in shops is imported from Spain where the little blighters are also an invasive species causing the same problems as they do in this country.

I was on the Thames at Abington waiting for upstream boats to clear the lock and on the bankside a man was unloading, from a flat-bottomed boat, a dozen crayfish pots all crawlingly full. I stopped to look at his catch.

'What do you do with them?' I asked.

'I spray them gold and silver and sell them as Christmas decorations,' he told me.

At the moment American Signal Crayfish may be public enemy number one but there are plenty of other invasive species on the waterways. EA notices on the River Nene warn of killer shrimps. As I cruise alone down the waterways should I worry about killer shrimps lurking beneath my boat? I have an image of killer shrimps rearing out of the water and theorising boaters.

The crayfish are thought to have escaped from farms set up to breed them for the restaurant trade. It is unlikely that animal rights activists set them free, unlike the minks, another invasive species from America, which now prowl the river banks. The signal crayfish just aren't the sort of animals that appeal to animal rights activists. They don't look pretty on posters.

Mink, however, do look pretty on the posters that decry the existence of mink farms and plead for the abolition of the fur trade. They are quite a common sighting on the river banks. I have seen them on numerous occasions on the Great Ouse and the Nene. I had always hoped that the furry animal that I had seen diving into holes in the riverbank or disappearing under water was an otter but in reality I know that it was likely to be the smaller, bolder mink. Walking along the banks of the Nene there was no doubt the sleek, black furred, weasel like creature walking towards me was a mink. I stopped stock still wishing not to frighten him but I needn't have bothered. He continued along the footpath passing within feet of me, giving me a disdainful look as he passed, then with one final glance he dived into the river, crossing to the other side in one quick, deft movement, came out of the water and strolled past a pair of surprised dog walkers. Although they are tough and voracious killers the minks are, surprisingly, on the decline. Cleaner water and the re-introduction of otters being given as the reason although maybe they have just eaten all the water voles and are running out of food. The Environment Agency would also like to eradicate the mink completely, they have managed to rid East Anglia of an estimated 200,000 coypu, also escapees from fur farms in the 1980's, so there must be hope that the mink may also be eradicated although the bigger, slower coypu must have been an easier target.

It's not only the foreign fauna that is the problem there is also a problem with invasive flora. It is especially a problem with plants that grow in and around rivers because they often spread using the flow of water to take plants and seeds many miles from the original plant. Japanese Knotweed is the most hated of these because it is so difficult to eradicate and it can cause so much harm to other species and even to the infrastructure of buildings. It is a reportable plant and the growing of it could be offence under the Antisocial Behaviour

Crime and Policing Act 2014. I just love the thought of an ASBO being slapped on a plant. I have a picture of the Japanese knotweed and, being a good citizen, I will phone the appropriate authorities (whoever they may be) if I spot some on the river banks although I'm not one hundred percent certain that I would identify it correctly. It may be best not to rely on me in the campaign to rid Britain of it.

I'm not sure I'd identify floating pennywort either, it's a plant of shallow water that multiples rapidly covering the surface. The lack of light can cause the death of native plant species; stop feeding insects from reaching the surface and in consequence harms the habitat and food supply of fish. It can cause problems to boaters by hampering air-cooled systems and becoming entangled in propellers. I've had enough problems with blanket weed enveloping the prop and making me grind to a halt so I don't need the additional hazard of floating pennywort. I'll report that as well if I manage to identify it.

Much easier to identify is the giant hogweed. As the name suggests it is big. In fact, compared to its close cousin the cow parsley, it is a giant. I have certainly seen some examples of this unwanted visitor along the waterways and, luckily, I have been safely on the boat not walking past it as touching the stems can cause severe skin burns.

Although the giant hogweed is impressive my favourite foreign invader is the Himalayan Balsam. It grows along the river banks and flowers in the summer and early autumn. It has small pink flowers and huge swathes of it can colonise the river banks. The seeds can drop into the water and flow downstream for miles before starting a new batch of balsam. It grows thickly, and the lack of light caused by this growth stops native species from thriving. In the winter it dies back leaving banks exposed and at risk of erosion. As Himalayan Balsam is an annual the best way to eradicate it is to cut it down before it has chance to flower and produce seeds. In areas where it has taken hold balsam bashing parties are held in the spring, the aim being to stop the flowering and thereby stop the spread of the plant.

Yet to cruise down a river or canal through a tunnel made of the dense clumps of Himalayan Balsam when dappled sunlight plays on the clusters of pink flower plants and insects and bees busy themselves amongst the plants is a delight. I know Himalayan Balsam is an antisocial plant and I shouldn't really enjoy it being there but it is so very, very pretty.

Going Swimmingly

My Nicholson's guide tells me that Lee Valley Leisure Pool at Broxbourne is a 'fine facility offering fitness suites, saunas and steam baths'. I'm moored only a few hundred yards from the site of the pool so I'm looking forward to a swim and a laze in a sauna although I might give the steam bath a miss. I pack costume, towels and shower equipment and trot off to find the pool. I find it gone. I wander around for a while across an area of landscaped paths and grassland, I consult the map frequently, I look at the Google map on my phone, I'm in the right place but the leisure centre isn't here. My waterways map is only a few years old so if it says there is a leisure centre here then here there must be a one. I'm used to my Nicholson's guide singing the praises of pubs which are now empty, boarded up or converted to flats. I have learned from bitter experience (or more likely a pint of bitter free experience) not to look forward to mooring up alongside a recommended pub because there is a strong likelihood the said pub closed down long ago. However, I would have thought leisure centres would have the decency to hang around a bit longer. There is a sense of permanence about leisure centres that the more frivolous pubs don't have.

As I journey along the canals and rivers I like to visit the swimming pools. When I was in Cambridge, moored at Jesus Green, my planned swim was again thwarted when I was told it was closed for the day while filming took place for a TV documentary on Barnes Wallis. He hadn't tested his bouncing bomb in the Jesus Green pool but it was the only remaining open air pool that was similar to where early testing took place. Later, when the pool had re-opened, I could see that the length of the pool would be useful for the testing of bouncing bombs. It was one short step for a bouncing bomb but one long swim for an overweight and unfit woman.

My visit to the pool in Marlow on the Thames was thwarted even more determinedly when I moored up on the bank a short walk away from the pool. To moor at the elegant towns of Marlow, Henley and Windsor is relatively expensive, especially as I had got used to the free mooring on the canals but at both Marlow and Windsor the mooring fee does include a swim session in their pool. To my mind that makes it well worth the money. I moored at Marlow, the last space on the long bank-side. I soon found out why that space was free: it was above an outlet of water. At frequent intervals a gush of bubbling water rumbled under the boat. It was loud and disturbing but there were no other moorings available and I'd paid my fee before I realised how disturbing this outlet of water was. Usually very little keeps me awake but this strange underwater eruption did and it also frayed my nerves. In the morning I looked forward to a long swim to ease the frazzled nerves only to be told that the swimming pool was closed that day for maintenance. I didn't take the news well; I had a hissy fit, stamped my feet and shouted at the two hapless pool receptionists who had nothing to do with the charging of mooring, the bubbling water outlet or the closure of the pool. It wasn't my finest hour.

After not finding a swimming pool at Broxbourne I discovered that Broxbourne didn't seem to do food shops either so, as I was planning on being in the area for a week or more, I turned around and moved back to Cheshunt alongside another part of the lovely Lea Valley Park where wooden sculptures lurk amongst the trees. I was opposite a water-sports centre where the squeals of children learning to canoe reverberated across the lake. Cheshunt has food shops and a useful railway station with trains that go to where I wanted to go. It also has a leisure centre which hasn't metamorphosed into an area of landscaped grassland. I stayed the ten days and managed plenty of swimming and walking in the Lee Valley Park.

On leaving Cheshunt and its modern swimming pool I progressed further up the Lee Valley to Ware where the charming 18th Century gazebos line the river and there is a 1930's Lido. In warm sunny weather, after the initial shock of plunging into cold water, an open-air swimming pool is a delight. I ploughed gently up and down the pool as the sun glittered on the water and warmed my shoulders.

Onwards from Ware into Hertford and their swimming pool was only a short walk from my river side mooring. I rested in the shallow end listening to the conversations of fellow swimmers.

'He said, they said he could speak at the planning meeting but he was only allowed to speak for three minutes. "I'll be speaking for two minutes," he said.

'Well I timed him and I said, "do you know Jim that was exactly two minutes."

'He said, "yes I know I've spent days standing in front of the microwave getting the timing right."

In my brief survey of the swimming pools along the Lee Navigation I have, unsurprisingly, to give the award for the best facility to the Olympic Pool at Stratford. I visited it with a degree of trepidation, expecting the other swimmers to be fit and healthy and doing lengths at the speed of sound. When I entered the area I was regaled by the comforting smell of chlorine and the echoing sound of the chatter of adults, the squeals of children and the splash of water. These are the smells and sounds of all indoor pools however grand their original use.

The Olympic pool is big and beautiful and the enjoyment of being there was enhanced by the knowledge of the record-breaking sporting feats achieved and the excitement generated during the 2012 Games. On the morning I visited there was the added bonus of pausing for breath between lengths and watching the perfectly honed body of Tom Daley repeatedly diving from the springboard.

Hertford and Back

On the way to Hertford, passing through Ware, I was told constantly that the gate at the lock into Hertford was damaged and was likely to be closed for a week. I was told about it so often that I began to think that a damaged lock was the most exciting thing that had happened to Hertford in years. There was an exodus of boats leaving Hertford before they were locked in because of the closure. A week's closure suited me fine, it meant I would be able to get a pleasant mooring next to the allotments in the town centre and a week or so without cruising meant that I would have a chance to catch up with friends and family and laundry.

As it happened the lock repairs were done in a few days and when Jessica joined me at Hertford for the cruise back to London they were open and I could turn around and go back the way I had recently come.

Jessica arrived by train early in the morning by four o'clock in the afternoon we had managed two locks, three miles and eight charity shops.

By eight in the evening we had increased our tally to another four locks and five miles and a pub and the only reason that our tally of charity shops remained at eight was because they had closed for the day.

I decided I was going to attempt to get to Limehouse Basin without stopping again because to the best of my knowledge there were no charity shops in Limehouse Basin for her to drag me into.

A difference of perceptions about spending money in charity shops: I thought she had spent £25, she thought she had saved £125.

By Saturday our intention was to leave our overnight mooring at Cheshunt and travel to Limehouse, stopping first at Hackney to have a walk around the Olympic Park. The start was delayed by rain then progress was slow as every lock was against us or we had to wait for boats approaching us to clear the locks. Jessica told me she thought the shiny brass mushrooms on the boats coming through the lock were garish. The dull and tarnished hue of mine was much more interesting; they had the patina of age (or more likely it was the patina of neglect). If she continues making comments like that she could stay a few more days. I might even go in another charity shop with her.

Approaching Enfield Lock we were informed by a boat heading upriver that C&RT had been called about low water levels. A man in a blue sweatshirt and orange life-jacket was hovering around the bridge but not taking any notice of us down in the lock. It took us a long time to fill the lock mainly because we hadn't noticed that one of the paddles downstream was open. Presumably the man in the blue sweatshirt and orange life-jacket was making an attempt to put more water into the very low basin between Enfield Lock and Pickett's Lock. With the paddle closed the lock filled more quickly and the river behind us emptied less slowly. It was then a crawl along a long and shallow pound where exposed mud banks lined the right-hand bank. I needed frequent blasts of reverse to remove debris from the prop. It is a waste of time and energy trying to put more revs on to try and increase speed in shallow water, it only seems to push more water under the bow, hammer the engine, make a lot more noise, and all the extra effort only makes the boat go slower. Jessica sat in the bow reading her book and I stood patiently, the gear in tick-over, my mind in neutral, watching the high banks of the reservoirs crawl slowly past.

When we reached Pickett's Lock there followed a period of puzzlement about how the automated locks worked and which one of the pair was the automated one, so this slowed our progress even more. It was only a few weeks since I passed this way but at my age short term memory loss is a problem. I expected the journey between the next locks to be better but it was another crawl along a shallow pound. The exposed mud banks, mottled with the prints of birds, embedded with various slime covered debris, glistened dully to my right.

It was getting too late to have a wander around the Olympic Park and still have time to move onto Limehouse Basin so once we were beyond Lea Bridge I started to look for a place to moor. Possible mooring places were nonexistent and once we were in sight of The Olympic Park the boats were not just moored bow to stern along the towpath but were also double parked. The few gaps between boats were too short for Rea and the chance of tying up anywhere along here appeared slight. I passed a space opposite a crowded outside bar and decided belatedly that it was just big enough for Rea to fit into. As I reversed back along the canal I said to Jessica, 'I have an audience, I bet I make a hash of this.' I did make a hash of it. I poked the stern in and she dismounted: I threw the centre rope: she missed it and the rope fell in the canal: I throw my second centre rope: she caught it and pulled. I walked down the gunwale to retrieve the first centre rope because I didn't want to risk it getting caught in the propeller yet again, but by this time the stiff breeze had caught the bow and the bow had made its way determinedly to the other bank. Jessica had sensibly let go of the rope instead of being pulled into the water. I retrieved both ropes but by that time I found that Rea was firmly wedged. My stern was against a moored boat on one side and my bow button was under the rather shaky wooden structures of the bar on the other. I was well and truly jammed so it was useless trying to reverse out. I walked along the gunwales to the bow and politely asked some personable young men if they would mind putting their craft beer down for a few minutes and help me extricate my button from under the bar. Reluctantly they did so. Trendy young men in trendy London bars aren't too keen to do anything (apart from a work-out at the gym) that might make them break into a sweat, look undignified or chip their manicured fingernails. Unsmilingly they leant over and pushed me free from the rather flimsy looking wooden platform which overhangs the river. Fortunately, I didn't take them or the bar with me. Free from the platform I beat as hasty a retreat as a narrowboat will allow. I didn't attempt a second shot of the mooring space opposite the bar or stop to pick up Jessica. Thankfully I found another space a few hundred yards further on and waited for her to catch up with me.

The towpath in Hackney Wick was heaving with people, the bars and bridges and streets were heaving with people. There was live music from the bar across the canal and lively music coming in from different directions. We asked one of the crowd why all the people were about and we were told it was The Hackney Wicked Festival. We decided the walk around the Olympic Stadium could wait until the following morning; we would rather stay here and partake of the Festival. We hadn't a clue what the Hackney Wicked Festival was about but hey a festival is a festival and we were going to join in.

We roamed amongst the young crowd who were drinking and eating at the mix of venues, ate some street food (South American for me in memory of Ecuador, balls for Jessica in memory of who knows what) but the studios and art installations were closing for the day and the bands were packing their bags and going home so we went back to the boat and sat in the bow to drink wine and people watch.

A young man stopped to ask if he could take a photo. 'Of course,' we said thinking, 'fame at last.' We put on our best photogenic smiles and reclined attractively against the cushions but he wasn't interested in photographing us, he asked us to put our glasses of wine next to the cheese, biscuits and grapes and photographed those instead. The wine and cheese were an emblem of our idyllic life-style he told us. Idyllic! He should photograph me grovelling in the weed-hatch on a cold, wet day clearing all the muck that the prop had picked up in a rubbish strewn canal and then see if he still thinks it is an idyllic life-style.

The next person that stopped by the boat didn't want to take our photos she just wanted to use the toilet. I hoped she wasn't a flamboyant flusher and didn't use an excessive amount of water by washing her hands extravagantly, as most land-based dwellers do, because the sewage tank was getting rather full and the water tank was getting rather empty.

Not Going on the Tideway

I had toyed with the idea of going on the tidal Thames to Teddington and beyond but I was rather undecided about whether I wanted to attempt the journey. To go under Tower Bridge, passed the Houses of Parliament and through to Richmond on the incoming tide sounded exciting. It also sounded scary. The Thames is a big river, there are big boats on it, the tides are strong and narrowboats are not made for deep waters; they are designed for flat and shallow canals. Also, although I have the requisite life-jackets and anchor I do not have a two-way radio which is also a must-have for all boats travelling along these tidal waters. Evidently mobile phones are not enough to summon help in an emergency. And if there is an emergency I am told that help arrives quickly; the Thames life-boat is the only life-boat station of the RNLI that has full time paid staff. The fact it has full-time staff is reassuring, the fact that it is the busiest life-boat station in the country is less reassuring. I do know that two boats from my mooring at Oundle were leaving on the afternoon tide and as both have a two-way radio, if I travelled with them, I wouldn't need to have a radio on my boat, and I would have company along the tidal waters. So, the company and the radio would solve one problem but it wouldn't solve the problem of me being a coward.

The dilemma to go or not to go solved itself when our lunch guests were over an hour late arriving and we didn't leave Hackney until it would have been time for me to set off from Limehouse on the afternoon tide. I arrived in Limehouse Basin just in time to slide into my friend's vacated places on the 24-hour moorings and to wave at them from a distance. We watched them bobbing along the Thames like a pair of match sticks on a large ruffled pond. They told me afterwards that the journey was rough, wind had whipped waves onto the Thames and the rib boats, taking paying customers for rides, constantly buzzed them. Spray blew over the top of the stern and bow and soaked the crew. Good job I didn't go then.

I watched the next batch of boats gathering in the large lock; three narrowboats all Rea look-a-likes (the same painted diamonds and doors) from Braunston. In centre of the boat sandwich was one manned by a single lady, of mature years, with only her dog for crew. She put me to shame. I was being wimpy about doing the trip with a boat load of people and she was setting sail with only a dog for company. Good on you lady on nb Charlotte; you are now my new role model.

The next boat to join them was a lone fifty-foot narrowboat from a hire company. A lad and his dad were on board. They didn't have any life-jackets, anchor or radio, they didn't seem to have a clue as how to steer the boat; they were not even sure which way to turn when the lock gates opened, yet they were happily going off on their jolly up the Thames.

The lock-keeper quizzed them about their equipment and gave them detailed information about what to do. She was obviously unhappy about letting them out and tried to dissuade them from travelling but she hadn't the authority to stop them. I didn't hear on the canal telegraph that there were any incidents on the river so presumably they reached their destination safely. It was not long after this that regulations were introduced that said hire-boats can only navigate the tidal Thames if there is a pilot on board.

When everybody had left and two flash cruisers had arrived, all without incident, we left for a walk along the fascinating back streets of the docklands area, where old converted warehouses loom overhead and new smart and expensive flats and historic pubs mingle amongst them. At St Katherine Docks the tourists and the locals were out in force and we sat amongst them on the dockside sipping cocktails and feeling as if we were on holiday as well.

Walking back along the Thames Path in evening sunshine the white outline of a large ship loomed close to the shore blocking the view through the alleyways that lead between the warehouses down to the river. It was The Silver Cloud a cruise ship heading for a berth above Tower Bridge. If monsters like that were travelling on the river I didn't want to be out there at the same time. I'm glad I stayed tied to the pontoon.

The next morning the intention was to set off early and progress through Central London but first I needed a pump-out and so I had to wait for the Marina office to open to buy a card. Card bought, engine started and I was ready to move over to the pump-out when a narrowboat chugged around from the marina and headed towards my space. He took an age getting into position, revved forwards and backwards but didn't make any progress, clipped a moored boat, almost got onto the landing and then drifted out again. There were now two other boats moored next to me. Us seasoned boaters stood and laughed and criticised and wondered why he was making such a meal of mooring on a small landing between two boats. It's not that difficult. We, of course, had never had to learn how to drive our boats, had never made mistakes, had never being made to look a fool by the wind. I made rude comments about his lack of ability, conveniently forgetting that only two days previously I completely blocked the Lee Navigation and nearly demolished a bar. While I was leaning on the boat laughing at his difficulties another narrowboat came around the corner to take my place in the queue at the pump-out. That served me right for making derogatory remarks about other people's boat handling skills.

At last, pumped out, we left and as we went through the first lock a man in a narrowboat waiting to come down said he was pleased to see two women handling a sixty-foot boat by themselves. He gave Jessica's arm an affectionate squeeze then leaned against a wall to watch her get on with wrestling the stiff lock gates. I suppose we women want equality so we can't moan when we get it.

We had the intention of going until we found somewhere to stop. The first space we found was just after the Islington Tunnel so we stopped for the night. The next morning a young man asked if I was staying for a few days and if so could I water his plants. After telling him I was leaving later that morning I then thought I could stay here for a few days, so I did. I didn't feel guilty about declining to water his plants because overnight the rain was very heavy and the herbs on my roof were having to learn to swim.

Blockages

I thought, maybe I'd stay on my Islington mooring for a few days or maybe I'd move. It all depended on weather, visitors, appointments, work and whether I could get around to making a decision. Then a family crisis meant the mooring's proximity to Kings Cross Station was helpful, so I decided to stay a few more days. Jessica left and a three days later Bob arrived. On Saturday my lunch guest, lurching off down the towpath at 9.00 pm turned back and shouted, 'You've got a bad problem with your toilet.' I'm sure the residents of the nearby flats, other boaters and the customers who were sitting on the terrace of the pub next to the bridge were all interested to know about the state of my toilet. I was surprised to find out about the state of my toilet because I'd only pumped it out on the previous Monday. The decision about moving on was made for me. I had to move to empty the toilet.

Boaters always say that when they get together, the talk always reverts to toilets. I'd lived on my boat for five years and never had a toilet conversation, maybe because I have never had a problem with the toilet. It seemed I'd got a problem now.

After torrential rain stopped, on a Sunday morning we set off for Little Venice and the pump-out facility. As usual it was busy, this must be the busiest sanitary facility and water point in the country on the busiest stretch of canal and it's located at a small space at the narrowest point of the canal where a bridge goes overhead and a large barge, used as a café, is moored. At the weekend, when many of the live-aboards are home from work and it is their moving day, it is exceptionally busy. You get to know fellow boaters by having complex discussions about the positioning of boats and who wants to use which of the utilities and how long each is going to stay. Eventually moored up at the pump-out, I put the card in the machine, the suction started and nothing happened, the gunge in the toilet stayed where it was. Was it the machine or me? I poked sticks in various orifices of the toilet system and the pump managed to remove two inches of nasty stuff before the machine timed out. We let a wide-beam onto the pump-out and they used two cards and reported that they didn't think the machine was working properly. I tried again with a fresh card, there was some movement but very little. I rang C&RT and reported a problem. I didn't really expect an immediate response on a Sunday but they said an engineer would come out and apologised that he would take about two hours to get there.

I tried clearing some of the blockage on my boat by pushing the toilet brush down the basin but the end of the brush dropped off and disappeared into the murk. The system would definitely be blocked now. Without going into too much yucky detail the only way forward was on with the marigolds and getting down and dirty. Let's just say I found the problem with my toilet and I blame my guests. I retrieved an awful lot of kitchen roll. Kitchen roll and toilets don't get on in the best of systems. Toilets that rely on a suction pump-out are most certainly not the best of systems and they defiantly don't like strong kitchen roll.

We waited patiently for the engineer to arrive, moving away from the pump-out for boats that needed to fill with water. I'd only filled the tank recently and didn't need water. I got into a minor dispute with a young lady on a boat double moored against the towpath who said I couldn't triple park. She backed down when I said I was only staying until the engineer arrived. I joined in a more heated dispute when same young lady wouldn't let another boater walk over her boat to access the rubbish bins because she had a baby on board. The argument was nothing to do with me but I was bored and thought a bit of confrontation helped pass the time waiting for the engineer. I asked her why if she was so concerned with double mooring and people crossing her boat she moored at Little Venice. She told me to mind my own business, she'd moor where she liked, she'd been living along this stretch of canal for seven years and I needn't think anybody was walking across her boat to get to the towpath. Maybe the birth of her baby had made her hormonal.

The engineer arrived in less than two hours and found the problem with the pump out machine, it was a faulty seal. Problem solved: the sewage tank was emptied and we went on our way, eventually finding a place to moor against another boat about a mile down the canal.

The first thing I needed after all the digging around in the toilet was a shower. I got into the shower soaped up and scrubbed, loaded my hair with shampoo and washed it vigorously and then the water stopped. I'd run out of water. This was despite spending four hours next to a water point and waving people onto the water point continually saying, 'It's OK, I don't need any water, we're only waiting for the pump-out.' Four bloody hours we were there moving backwards and forwards, annoying the neighbours and just sitting waiting. Four bloody hours when I could have filled the tank four times over! So, do I blame guests for my lack of water as well as my blocked toilet, did I have a boat load of flamboyant flushers and extravagant showers or was it just my usual level of vagueness about the state of the utilities on my boat?

I removed the soap and shampoo as best I could with the cold water from my emergency bottle. Bob had decided after all the chatting to passers-by and other boaters and all the button pushing he had been doing he needed a shower as well. We explained to the nice young couple in the boat we had moored against, and who had helped tie us securely onto the bank and their boat, that we wouldn't, after all, be staying. Then it was off back to the water point. We cast off, went down the canal to the next turning point and did an interesting turn against a gale force wind that had sprung up from nowhere. Somewhere on the journey to the turning point my tablecloth on the bow table (£3.50 from one of my many visits to charity shops in Hertford) blew away. The way the day had been going I thoroughly expected to get it wrapped around my prop on the way back. I didn't. If another boat picks it up around their prop I sincerely apologise and if it isn't too shredded can I please have it back because it matches my paintwork. Then we were back in Little Venice spending an hour and a half in gathering darkness filling the water tank (slow tap: thin hose: large tank).

In the last week I had spent more money on my sewage system than I had on wine so, in an attempt to redress the balance, I went to Sainsbury while the water tank was filling. Sainsbury was closed. I went on to M&S in Paddington and on the way there I spotted a free slot in Paddington Basin. By the time the water tank was filled darkness had descended and in a howling gale we went around to Paddington Basin and did a wind assisted mooring on the one, luckily still available, space.

I stayed on that mooring for over two weeks, with full permission from C&RT. My ex-husband who had been taken ill a few days previously sadly died and I needed to spend time with my children over this difficult period.

Safety and Security

Bob is a lot more conscious of security than I am. Doors are always locked when he leaves the boat; windows closed; belongings moved from under the cratch cover; tools brought in from on top of the roof. I don't do any of this. To my mind he is too obsessed with security. He thinks under every canal bridge there lurks a potential thief, that the towpaths are full of 'ne'r do wells' as he calls them, and every passing boat is likely to stop so the thieving crew can drain off my diesel. He could be right, he has been boating on these canals and rivers for a lot more years than I have. The many instances of dishonesty he has encountered and the tales he has heard must have engendered a sense of mistrust.

But I still think he is too security conscious. I told him off, in no uncertain terms, one night when he decided to fix the large padlock to the outside of the stern door simply because he thought we were in an unsavoury area. I think it is more dangerous to be unable to get out of the stern door in the case of emergency than it is to allow thieves and vagabonds to come in.

He got told off again, when we were packing up because I was intending to leave the boat alone in Perivale for a week. He started removing the spare ropes from the roof. I had to carefully explain my policy of leaving the boat looking as if I have just walked out to the shops for ten minutes rather than having left it alone and unguarded for ten days.

He points out that ropes are expensive and easily stolen and it is not much of an effort to remove them.

I took him along the line of boats and pointed out the ones that had been left. They were the boats with tightly closed curtains and roofs bereft of belongings. They were the ones with the chimney stack taken inside. They were the ones with large padlocks securing the outer doors. They may have signs in the window saying, 'There is no money on board and we have drunk all the alcohol' but a boat still has valuable mechanical things on board, batteries or generators and diesel in tanks. It may simply have something that somebody needs. The only item that has gone missing from my boat was the coolie hat from above the central heating vent. It couldn't have blown off or been scraped off when I miscalculated the height of a low bridge (as was my chimney pot) because it was too securely fixed. Somebody unscrewed it and took it. It wasn't the crime of the century but it was annoying. I had to order a new one because the marinas I passed didn't stock them. Hanging around waiting for a delivery wasn't really convenient when I wanted to be on the move. I did think of keeping a look-out for an unattended boat with the same Aldi outlet and stealing theirs but that would have been mean.

I leave the ropes and the boating paraphernalia of boat hooks, poles and planks on the roof. I leave a few tea towels hanging on the line in the bow and I only close the curtains on the towpath side. If there isn't a lot of rain forecast I leave the cratch covers open because my theory is that a closed cratch cover gives a potential thief the cover he (or even she if I am being even handed with gender) needs when breaking down the door. I do think I went a bit too far with my 'leave it as if you've just gone out' approach when I left the boat near Camden Lock for five days with the keys still sitting in the door but the boat and the keys and all my personal possessions were still there when I got back.

As with many of my theories these theories on boat security are as much to do with bone idleness and forgetfulness as with safety. I really can't be bothered to remove ropes and boards, to check every window and lock every door every time I leave the boat. It takes me all my time to summon the energy to switch off the gas, electricity and water. Even if I'd taken every security measure possible my boat is still easy to break into. The bolts on the hatch wouldn't resist a lot of force, the front door has a weak lock and the windows could easily be broken or removed.

My main acknowledgment to security is to leave the boat where I feel it is safe. If I have a bad feeling about an area I don't moor there. I try to moor where there are people about, where other boats are moored and, if I am in an urban area, where there are security cameras. I will often tell other moorers that I am going to be away for a few days, although I'm not sure that is sensible. I am assuming that other boaters

237

are not likely to take advantage of my absence although logically who else would want a nice set of centre ropes or a new fender. I am rather like my mother who, when we were on the beach at Bridlington, would ask the family in the next cluster of deck chairs to, 'keep an eye on our things' as we went down to the sea. She never thought that we may be sitting next to the biggest bucket, spade and towel thieves in the country; she presumed if they were sitting on the beach next to us they must be honest. I work on a similar principal; I presume if the inhabitants of the boat moored next to me are a pleasant middle-aged couple with ample girths they must be honest. It never enters my head that they may fund their drug habit by syphoning off diesel and selling it off cheaply or run a black market in boat poles. On the other hand, I would never ask people in the local pub to keep an eye on my boat because I'm going away. In my view people in pubs can't be trusted; people in boats can. In fact, other boaters do work on the same theory as me: a person lives on a boat therefore they must be honest. I have been asked to watch boats because people were away for a few days. I've been given telephone numbers in case of problems, on two occasions. I've been asked to water plants on the roof of a boat when their owner was going to be absent and once a stranger left me her keys so I could feed her cat when she had to go to a funeral.

When I left my boat at Waltham Forest for three weeks, other boaters obviously clocked an unattended boat because when I came back I had three different people enquiring if I was the rightful owner. So even if you don't ask fellow moorers to look after a boat they still do, it is one of the delightful aspects of being on the water.

My way of leaving a boat in a place with which I feel comfortable and looking as if I am returning to it shortly seems to work. I left my boat in Ware for a few days. I'd had reports about boat break-ins in Ware so I left it in a busy spot under a surveillance camera and returned a few days later to find windows and possessions intact. The next morning I shared a lock with a man who was taking his boat to Stansted Abbot for repairs. He said his window had been smashed, his boat broken into, stereo and computer equipment taken and a thousand pounds worth of cash stolen (would anybody leave a thousand pounds worth of cash on an unattended boat?) He had been moored two boats further along from me. Maybe he was unlucky and I was just fortunate that the perpetrators hadn't moved on along the towpath and broken into my boat. Maybe it was that I didn't have any cash or computers on board. Or more likely it was because I hadn't been in the local pub boasting about my state-of-the-art stereo equipment and telling them that I was going to Spain for four days, as my travelling companion admitted he had done.

I felt my security policy was vindicated when I read the advice from C&RT which said that it was best not to make it too obvious that a boat had been left alone for a long period. Don't remove all the usual boating equipment of boats and poles from the roof and don't fit large, noticeable padlocks to external doors. It added that on no account should padlocks be fitted to rear external doors while the owners slept on board as this would block the rear exit and, in event of fire or sinking, could prove fatal. However, they didn't go as far as to suggest leaving the keys in the lock when moored alongside a busy towpath.

Part Six – Ambling Around

Urban Wildlife

Waking up moored on the Grand Union Canal near Perivale on New Year's Day, I could hear the chatter of parakeets. After a night of celebrating the start of the New Year one does doubt one's senses but as I surfaced tenderly from sleep I knew it was definitely parakeets that I could hear. Across the canal in the trees on the golf course a raucous flock of green ring-necked parakeets were exacerbating the hangovers of the residents of West London. I shouldn't have been surprised to hear these birds shrilly calling for there are an estimated 30,000 parakeets in the London area and I had recently seen flocks in Kew Gardens and Greenwich Park. These bright green birds are a very attractive sight but they are noisy. They are on the cusp of becoming a problem, a problem that may have a natural solution. As the number of parakeets increases so does the number of their predators: peregrine falcon and sparrow hawk numbers are on the increase in the area. There are now two breeding pairs of the rarer, migratory hobbies in Kensington Gardens that mainly feed on dragon flies, large insects and small birds. Analysis of the droppings of these raptors have shown that green ring-necked parakeets are often their luncheon of choice.

On leaving that mooring at Perivale, to head out of London, ploughing through thin ice which crackled under the bow I kept a look-out for two large terrapins. These are more or less a permanent feature sitting on the bows of a tree which overhangs the water just beyond the road bridge. They weren't sitting on their usual branch; hopefully they were only hibernating for the winter and will be back in place if I pass by again in the summer.

There is a lot of wildlife in the centre of large urban conurbations. In my daughter's garden in London, which looks out onto a small park, I can see a greater variety of wild life than I can see in many country places: a multitude of squirrels, woodpeckers and jays and foxes. Coming back late at night, to my boat moored amongst the high-rise offices and the hospital complex at Paddington Basin, I came face to face with a fox. He slunk into a doorway as I walked past him and after I'd crossed the bridge I turned to watch him. He was striding purposefully along the walkway, turned blue at intervals as the security lights alongside the jetty illuminated him. Urban foxes are a mangy looking lot compared to their sleeker, fitter country cousins. Obviously their diet of chips and MacDonald's throwaways aren't as good for them as their natural diet of rabbits and chickens. They are an increasing nuisance in cities foraging in bins and breeding in gardens, there have even been reports of babies bitten as they slept. If the Quorn Hunt could be persuaded to keep a pack in London and hunt regularly along the streets of Bermondsey I'm sure many of the residents would support the Countryside Alliance in their move to bring back hunting with dogs.

Yet I always think the animal who has adapted best to urban living is the little black and white coot. You can't take a coot seriously there's that name for a start; coot not the most sophisticated of names. Then there's the feet; large white skeletal feet, at least three sizes too big for their slim, streamlined bodies. And, in addition, there are the chicks; little, vocal, black scraps of fluff with a silly ginger top-knot.

But mostly it's their nests which are the cause of amusement; edifices made up of all the urban rubbish that flows along the canals and rivers. The coots build their, often towering, structures in corners of buildings, alongside jammed logs and in the tyres that have been strung alongside boats to be used as fenders. Over-stayers on the canals love coots, they encourage them to build their nests on the rear fender, hatch out a brood of chicks and then the boater can tell C&RT 'sorry we'd love to move on but we can't because we've got a family of coots nesting on the propeller.'

The spring I was flood-bound on the River Nene, a wren built a nest in the rolled-up nook of my cratch cover. I didn't realise it was there and I unfurled the cover, tragically displacing the nest and causing the three tiny, pale blue eggs to smash on the gunwales of the boat. It was a delicate, intricate woven nest with a down lining. It was an exquisite example of the skilful workmanship of a bird. A coot's nest could never be described as exquisite and most certainly isn't a delicate structure. Yet on city canals and in quiet redundant docks a coot's nest is an edifice to admire. Made from twigs and leaves, from crisp packets and cigarette packets, from polythene bags, from drinks containers and food trays they utilise every bit of rubbish a well-abused canal has to offer. Unlike the neat little wren they don't work to a set design and construct a nest sufficient for their requirements. The more rubbish on offer that coots can collect the bigger the nest they can make and then defend aggressively against all comers. For coots are renowned for being aggressive little birds; they are also, like the cuckoo, parasitic. They don't lay their eggs with gay abandon in the nest of any bird, as the cuckoo does, they only lay eggs in the nests of their own species. Coots are also reported to be one of the few species of birds able to recognise their own young. When the usurpers eggs hatch they will sometimes recognise the chick as an intruder and kill the youngster. Coots are not as silly as they appear. Or as sweet.

One Saturday morning I was sitting in the bow of the boat in Little Venice. On the opposite side of the canal, in a tyre strung alongside a house-boat, a pair of coots and their one remaining off-spring, a scraggy teenager, had made their own des res in this most desirable part of London. It was a mass of twigs and leaves with crisp packets and scraps of paper stuffed in amongst them, no available piece of passing litter had gone to waste. The pride of place on the top of the nest was given to a food container. The problem with this nest, topped with waste, built on a busy canal was that passing boats created a wash. The wash displaced the crisp packets, the polythene bags and that precious food container. The three coots had their work cut out keeping their nest in order. They just stopped for a rest from their foraging when another boat passed by and the wash removed the top part of the nest. One of them had to go scuttling along the canal to bring the errant bit back and pass it up to the coot on top of the nest for that bird to return it to its prescribed place. Watching them at work kept me entertained for hours. Eventually a wide-beam boat passed by, dislodging the food container and dragging it behind in its wake. The son of the coot family hurriedly chased it, the young bird's big feet slapping along the surface of the water as he almost ran down the canal. He reached the container and dragged it back, passed my boat and home to the nest. This was no mean feat as the container was bigger than the young coot. He then valiantly heaved it onto the top of the nest, pushed it into its rightful place amongst the twigs and debris and stepped back to admire his handiwork.

Now that is another reason to really admire coots, not only can they usefully re-cycle all the rubbish in the canals but they can also get their teenage son to tidy his own bedroom.

Continuous Stopping

It was my first winter as a continuous cruiser. Muddy towpaths, dark nights, cold days. Drizzle and damp mornings. It wasn't a bad winter as winter's go. I just wished it would go. I visited friends more often than they deemed necessary. I stayed with my daughter in London and when the opportunity came to accompany a friend to Colombia for her son's wedding, I grabbed it.

I made my way slowly and coldly along the canal, staying in places where there is a convenient rail link; Uxbridge, Rickmansworth and Croxley Green. Some days when I was moving the boat I became so cold that when I reached my intended destination my legs could hardly get me off the boat and my fingers were so numb they wouldn't tie any of the ropes. I tried to avoid using locks on icy mornings in case I slipped and fell in the water. I was wearing so many layers of clothes that if I did fall in I'd sink without trace.

By Croxley Green I felt I was gradually leaving the sprawl of London behind. Watford was somewhere to my left but it didn't impinge on the canal. I moored up in a quiet spot with only a wide-beam boat a few slots ahead of me. The spot wasn't as quiet as I thought for the wide-beam had a group of friends on board intent on doing some serious partying until the early hours of the morning. The next day the owner came and apologised for all the noise but, as I explained, they needn't have bothered apologising, they'd moored away from other boats, it was me who'd moored in the same vicinity. I only hoped they'd enjoyed themselves. From the look on his face I think he'd enjoyed the night but he wasn't enjoying the morning after very much.

Trees lined the cut here. On that sunny Sunday in February I tried to find a pathway to Watford underground station, one of the last stations on the Metropolitan Line, but I didn't seem to take the right pathway. After a few hours of more trees, more pathways, meeting families out for a Sunday stroll and fit people out for a run I gave up and felt glad to simply find my way back to the canal and my warm boat. Progressing further along the canal it threaded through peaceful Cassiobury Park under the white and elegant Lady Capel's Bridge and through a manicured golf course. It felt very pretty and rural here, even though busyness was only a mile or so away from the tranquillity. I stopped at Hemel Hempstead for a week, opposite the railway station. I moan about the juxtaposition of the canal and the railway when high speed trains are roaring past and spoiling the quietness of the day but this proximity is acceptable when I need a train to get to London. I moved on from Hemel and stopped a few locks further on and then couldn't find my keys to operate the Winkwell Swing Bridge. The curse of Winkwell strikes again! I remembered the last time I had them was to use the key at a waterpoint, I walked back and scratched and scraped in the grass alongside the dripping tap but there was no sign of them. It was okay though I still had the spare I bought last year. Two days later I found the keys in my dressing gown pocket. I'm not sure how they got there. I certainly wasn't wearing my dressing gown when I filled the tank at the water-point.

I moored up at the affluent, historic market town of Berkhamsted. The town is interesting and the shops are individual but rather pricey, in fact I couldn't even afford the charity shops in Berkhamsted. The remains of the Norman motte and bailey castle rise above the useful railway station. Around the edges of the moat, daffodils were starting to bloom. I was moored within sight of the castle walls, outside a pub with walks into town, around the castle or along the canal. There was even a Waitrose supermarket nearby and from the other side of the canal a large totem pole kept guard over me.

I got the train to London to spend the weekend with my daughter. When I arrived on King's Cross station my name was called over the tannoy. After a few minutes with a panicking, fluttering stomach I found the guard only to be told that I'd left my handbag on Berkhamsted station. With no money, no Oyster card and no phone I couldn't continue my journey. The guard kindly let me on the train back to Berkhamsted where I collected my handbag and got back on the next train to London arriving only three hours behind schedule.

As a frequent forgetter of phones, loser of keys and bags, miss-placer of tickets I am genuinely surprised and pleased at how honest and helpful most people are. I've had purses with money intact handed in to the police. I've had my keys retrieved in Ely and on the canal system and messages passed along the linear telegraph system of the waterways about their whereabouts. The only thing I didn't get back was a brand new pair of shoes left on the station platform in Cambridge. I still bemoan their loss. Maybe the most surprising retrieval of belongings was a tatty old rucksack left on the station platform at Stratford, I never thought that anybody would want it but I did think it may be a security risk. I realised as soon as I got on the train that I'd left it behind. Worried about the bag causing a security alert I tried to call Stratford but nobody answered. At the first stop I got the attention of a guard and told him about the lost bag. At my destination I went into the ticket office and the assistant tried to call Stratford but to no avail. I spent the next few hours monitoring the news bulletins for security alerts on the rail network. There weren't any. A week later after fruitless calls to the lost property offices along the rail network I was again in Stratford and asked a guard where they would put lost property.

'We sometimes put it in a shed,' he said. 'Follow me.'

I followed him, over bridges, down passages, along walkways to a small shed at the end of an isolated platform. He opened the door and there was my old grey rucksack. There were other bags there as well. To my undiscerning eye

250

many of them had the potential to contain bombs. I thanked the guard profusely then scuttled of hurriedly down the platform before the shed exploded behind me.

I would have been happy to stay in Berkhamsted longer but I needed to move onwards and upwards to Milton Keynes.

At the end of March, the days lengthened but it didn't get any milder. I didn't mind too much as I would gladly trade daylight for warmth. My progress continued slowly: work in London intervened; visits to family; a short stay in Italy. To give me the ability to escape the boat I collected my car from my friend's drive and dragged it along behind me. Not literally, of course. I'd park up, move the boat and after a few days get train, bus or use my legs to go back and collect the car and park it somewhere near the boat. It gave me something to do and it meant I could explore areas beyond the canal.

That year the intention was to go North, up the River Soar then turn onto the Trent heading through Nottingham and Newark. A bit of a detour towards York and then come back on the Leeds and Liverpool. That's as far as the planning went. I hadn't worked out where to go after Liverpool. I planned not to work for a few months I'd just concentrate on boating. And Bob was coming with me. I'm not doing all those locks by myself.

251

The Leicester Branch

By April I was onto the familiar ground of Stoke Bruerne. Once more I'd passed my planned detours down the Aylesbury Arm and the Wendover Arm. I'd do them the next time I came this way. I gritted my teeth for a drive through the long, dark, dripping Blisworth tunnel. Nothing happened, no other boats, no bouncing off walls, no problems but I still hate tunnels.

Then I jettisoned the car. It was taken back to my friend's drive in Cambridge and I got a lift back to the boat. This symbolic act made me feel as if I was eventually going on my travels, I'd always felt a bit fraudulent boasting of being a continuous cruiser when I had a car and escape route parked just around the corner. To be a true nomad of the waterways I felt I shouldn't have a useful car nearby. I should be carrying shopping in a large back-pack and never venturing off the boat to go anywhere that wasn't on a bus-route.

Bob came on board so although I was now a bona-fide continuous cruiser I was no longer a bona-fide single-hander.

After the Buckby Flight we turned right to go down the Leicester Arm towards the flight of the seven manned staircase locks at Watford Gap. We went under the A5 and then ran alongside the M1. It was noisy. Watford Gap is a gap between two hills. The A5, the M1, the railway and canal are all squeezed into its narrow space. We moored up and I walked up the steep sides of the flight of locks to find the lock-keeper. During the summer months boaters have to book in with the lock-keepers who monitor the flow of traffic and make sure people like me don't get the sequence of opening and closing the gates wrong. Getting the sequence wrong empties all the side pounds instead of filling the locks. We had to wait for three boats to come down the flight and while waiting I found a gap in the hedge and went to the Watford Gap service station to buy milk. If I thought the canal was noisy a quick visit to a busy motorway service station soon put things into perspective.

The passage up the seven locks only took half an hour. Once on the summit it's a twenty-mile lock-free stretch before we reached the downward flight at Foxton. Apart from the nasty, wet tunnel that got in the way at Crick it would have been my idea of perfect, leisurely boating. It was twenty miles of varying shades of green, interspersed with yellow clumps of bog iris and pink straggles of dog roses climbing amongst the trees. Through the dense, lush vegetation of trees and ancient hedgerows, verdant hills, dotted with white sheep, climbed away from the canal. Green wheat fields cut with deeper, darker pattern of tractor tracks; fledgling drilled crops in neat bright rows against black earth. Curved brick bridges

253

crossed the canal from green field to green field. Few roads; no signs of habitation; no SMS signal. Somewhere nearby there is a railway hidden in a valley for the occasional screech of a train drowned out the sound of birdsong.

Then we reached Foxton. Despite all my proclamations about wanting an easy lock-free boating life I love the passage down the ten staircase locks at Foxton. It's the longest flight of staircase locks on the canal system yet the navigating of the ten locks isn't a mammoth task. For one thing with staircase locks you move from one lock directly into the next. With the two sets of five locks at Foxton there are twelve gates to open and close instead of the twenty that would be found on a standard flight of locks. The locks are single, well maintained and the paddles are easy to operate, and the gates well-balanced. Plus the locks are manned and there are additional volunteers on hand to help. It is also a busy visitor's area, with its pubs, café and adequate parking, a museum and the remnants of the Foxton inclined plane. Plenty of visitors means plenty of helpers to heave on the gates to open them, especially during school holidays and at weekends.

The inclined plane which runs alongside the canal was only operational for ten years in the early 1900's and only the basic structure of the ramp is left. Looking at it I think it must have operated something like the water shoot in East Park that I loved as a child. Put a boat at the top; attach a strong wire; let it go so it arrives at the bottom with a splash. With much raising of eyebrows and heavy sighing Bob demolishes this theory. What happened to the cargo on this steep downhill descent? What happened to the owner's possessions? What happened to the baby in its cot? Did the bargees need to purchase a new set of crockery every time they were despatched down the hill to land with a thump in the water at the bottom? Okay so it wouldn't work like that. Evidently the workings all had to do with equally weighted tanks of water and a gentle, even progression up and down the hill on a platform that took the boats. It's a good job I didn't decide to go for a career in engineering.

We had hoped to go down the flight the afternoon following our ascent of the Watford Flight but due to late setting-off, filling with water and general leisurely boating it was quite late in the day when we arrived and there was a queue to use the locks. We had to wait until the following morning to descend. This is one of the reasons the inclined plane was built; in busy times both Foxton and Watford Locks were bottle-necks, the ascent and descent taking up to an hour at each point. The locks, being single locks, restricted it to boats with a 6ft 10in beam and the wait in the queue to use them could be long. It matters little to leisure boaters (except hire boats who are on a tighter schedule) but for the working boats of the past, time lost was money lost. The workings of the inclined plane also saved much water usage. As can be imagined the continuous emptying of locks at Watford and Foxton could drain even a twenty-mile section of canal quickly.

The following morning when we booked the slot for the passage down, we were eighth in the queue and there were only three boats waiting to come up. The lock-keeper has to work out the best formula for getting boats up and down efficiently, bearing in mind that the water usage should be kept to the minimum. As in the locks at Watford, the system of emptying and filling the locks uses side pounds and it is essential to empty into the side pound and fill from the lock above in the correct sequence. I haven't totally grasped the engineering of this but I do know it's very clever. There are two paddles on each lock, one painted red, one painted white. I may only have operated the Watford flight two days previously but I did need reminding about the sequence. To help boaters remember there is an oft quoted rhyme; 'red before white and it's all right, white before red and you're dead.' At least I think that's what it is, it might be the other way around. When we took our turn to go down the flight I wielded the windlass, Bob drove and there was a volunteer lock-keeper to shout at me when I was too busy talking to spectators and headed towards the wrong paddle. The last time I came through Foxton Locks, it was with friends; they did the work (which isn't hard) and I talked to the visitors, and enjoyed displaying my knowledge, my driving skills and the proud ownership of my lovely boat. Now it's Bob that's answering all the questions. I want to shout, 'It's my boat, I'm capable of handling it myself!' Not that Bob ever claims ownership of the boat but I wouldn't like any of these people, that I'll never meet again, to assume that it belongs to him.

From the summit of Foxton locks the view is over open, rolling countryside; there are gentle hills, chequered fields and green woodland. It is lovely to ascend the locks and watch this attractive vista open up gradually. Although the

256

descent through the locks is not as scenic, it does have the tempting sight of the two pubs at the bottom of the flight.

At the end we turned right and headed down the six-mile length of the Market Harborough Arm which leads (unsurprisingly) into the Market Harborough Basin. The area around the basin, which used to be industrial, has been developed. The warehouses have been converted to flats, restaurants and craft units. The basin has mooring facilities but there was no room so we turned and moored back along the arm. Market Harborough is an attractive market town but it was the proximity of the station and not the charm of the elegant main street that had drawn me there. Bob headed home and I headed towards work in London.

Leicester

Up towards Leicester. From Market Harborough Basin we progressed through more empty, gentle Leicester countryside. Then suddenly into the outskirts of the city of Leicester. The recommended mooring in Leicester is at Castle Park. The secure moorings are on the non-towpath side of the river and have locked gates that are only accessible with a BW (the now defunct British Waterways) key. Such are the dire warnings, from other boaters, about crime and vandalism in Leicester that it would seem this is the only possible place to moor. To tie up anywhere else in the city is to risk, at the best, serious damage to the boat and theft of all moveable possessions and at the worst serious injury from marauding locals. When we arrived in Leicester all the moorings on Castle Park were taken. I suppose it would be possible to double moor but the first boat in the line had a sign in its window saying 'No mooring alongside.' I was torn between mooring alongside just to annoy them and keeping as far away as possible because they are obviously not the sort of people I'd wish to be in close proximity to. What we actually did is take advantage of the mooring rings on the boat free towpath side of river and tie up there. It is a wide walkway, well-lit and with a constant footfall. My 'don't moor here antennae' couldn't discern any potential problems. That day and night there weren't any problems and when boats moved away from the castle moorings the next morning I didn't see the need to take their place. Coming home late at night I prefer to walk along well-lit roads rather than through a quiet park. In any case it would be likely that I'd misplace my keys and be locked out when all other boaters were safely in bed and couldn't hear my shouts and rattling of the gate.

I was told that Leicester has a good market: the largest outdoor covered market in Europe. The market was interesting but when I visited, it was in a period of flux as a new indoor market was being built and I think something of the noise and vibrancy that one associates with city markets was lost. Leicester has a high Asian population yet in the market I wasn't as aware of this diversity of culture as I had been in Birmingham's wonderful market. I would like to see Leicester's market when all is finished and it has settled down, or what I would really have liked is to have seen it 700 years ago when the market first started trading on this site. That must have been fascinating.

As well as a market what Leicester has got is Richard III. It's had him for a long time, well over 500 years, but his body has only just been discovered bundled into a small grave under a unkempt car-park. Leicester is working on the principle of 'finders, keepers.' They found the body so they will keep it, despite challenges from York Minster and Westminster Abbey. To be fair Leicester needs the remains and the publicity more than either Westminster Abbey or York. Westminster Abbey is crammed with dead monarchs and their consorts; the remains of Richard III would be lost amongst all the other tombs and burial places. York, where it is reported that Richard III, a member of the House of York, expressed a wish to be buried has more than its fair share of tourist attractions and tourists. Although the magnificence of York Minster would seem to be a more appropriate resting place for a king, I hope Richard is happy here in this smaller, quieter, less imposing church.

I walked through the well-kept Castle Gardens and down to the Cathedral, it was early on a Tuesday morning and the air felt fresh. Around the open Cathedral Square, it was warm and welcoming. Here amongst the old buildings and the solid Victorian brickwork there is none of the bustle and rush that one associates with a large city. I spent the morning ambling around, visiting the tomb of Richard III where it has been re-interred in the nave of the cathedral. I visited the newly opened Richard III visitors centre and found out much about English history that I should have known but didn't, plus about the diligence and hard work of the academics and members of the Richard III society in their successful quest to find the body.

It has always been known the body of Richard III was brought to Leicester after the Battle of Bosworth and that he spent a night before the battle here but otherwise he had very little connection with the area. Yet the finding of the twisted body with a hole in the skull has rejuvenated this area of the town. They have gone Richard III crazy. A Victorian school which was empty and dilapidated has been turned into the smart visitors centre because of the find. The black and white timber framed building near the cathedral boasts an exhibition 'Leicester in the time of Richard III'. As I started to walk back to the boat two coaches drew up, ready to disgorge their passengers into the Richard III experience. A crocodile of green-sweatered children chattered past, representing the cultural diversity of Leicester that I had failed to find in the market.

There is a plaque on the pretty Victorian Bow Bridge, which is decorated with the red and white roses of the houses of York and Lancaster. The plaque commemorates the passage of Richard III to the battle at Bosworth. Legend said that the King's remains were thrown into the River Soar from the original mediaeval stone bridge on this site. Subsequent events have proved this legend to be erroneous. Although it wouldn't be surprising if they had thrown his bones over the bridge, the residents of Leicester seem to throw most of their other rubbish into the river. As we left Leicester the section of river we passed through was clogged with debris of all description. I frequently put the gear into neutral to try and drift through the rubbish without getting any caught in the propeller, or into reverse to dislodge rubbish that did get caught. When I went down into the weed hatch to check what rubbish I'd picked up I found a plastic bag and a large fragment of a red and gold sari. I pulled it out, hoping the wearer wasn't attached to the rest of the sari.

As we left Leicester, going past the white futuristic building of the National Space Centre, (another place I've always intended to visit) we were now travelling, mainly, on the River Soar. Until this point the canal and river had run alongside each other or they intertwined, now until we reached the Trent most of the waterway is a river. When I came up the Soar, two years previously, there had been a lot of rain and the river had been on yellow boards, meaning that boaters should take care in the strong flows (if it had been red travel it would have been dangerous to travel). This time the river was on green boards meaning the river was low and slow but I still didn't like the long, unprotected weirs of the Soar. Last time I had been travelling upstream which made it easier to avoid the pull of the weir. This time I was travelling downstream and although the river levels were normal and the weirs were benign the sight of them and the promise of more to come still made me nervous.

At the end of the Soar where it joins the Trent there is a cut off which flows over an extensive weir, as I was approaching it I worried about that as well. What if my engines failed? What if my prop became entangled in rubbish and I couldn't steer? What if I take the wrong turn and simply drove over the weir? Of course, nothing happened, the weir is well signed and protected and I went past it and merrily on my way to the Trent.

The Erewash

Once again, work, visitors and my social life intervened with my plans to keep cruising and I needed to leave the boat for ten days. I made the decision to go up the Erewash canal and hoped to find a place there which was suitable for leaving the boat. Although the plan was to head up towards Nottingham and proceed northwards, my experience of rivers told me that finding a safe place to leave a boat for nearly two weeks might be difficult. Moorings on rivers tend to be few and far between and are only for a short period of time.

Also neither Bob or I had ventured down the Erewash so it was a new canal to explore and near the top end at Langley Mill, is Eastwood, the birthplace of D. H. Lawrence. I wanted to see the museum dedicated to him.

We went straight across the Trent river, through the Trent Lock and passed the busy boating centre beyond the lock and onto the Erewash canal. After that, apart from a Christian Boaters Rally at a canal-side pub, we hardly saw a boat.

There are twelve miles and fourteen locks of the Erewash canal which was originally built to take coal from the mines of Nottinghamshire and Derbyshire to The Trent and beyond. The first part of the canal runs through the towns of Long Eaton, Sandiacre and Ilkeston. In between there are short passages of open countryside. By the time we got to the atmospherically named Gallows Inn Lock I was getting a bit fed up of the Erewash and was thinking maybe we should have turned left on the Trent and headed towards Shardlow. There were two C&RT maintenance men at the lock and they offered to work the lock for us. Did we want the water let in gently or did we prefer 'the full Alton Towers experience?' they asked. After six miles and eight stiff locks I was in need of a bit of excitement so I went for the 'full Alton Towers' and they wound the paddles vigorously, the water gushed in and the boat bounced around. After that we went back to being unexcited as we carried on up the canal.

The good news was that the Great Northern Basin, where the Erewash and the disused Cromford and Nottingham canal joined together, is very civilised. It must be thought an achievement for boats to have got that far because boaters can get a certificate or plaque to prove that they have traversed the length of the Erewash. The bad news was that the moorings are for a limited time and if I was to leave the boat for the number of days I wished to be there then I would be over-staying. I walked back down the canal to see if there was any suitable place to safely moor the boat and three teenagers, who were fishing, thought it would be fun to follow me, shout abuse and try to throw maggots down my neck. Boys seem to do that when they are bored with fishing. I thought it wasn't the type of place I wanted to leave my boat. We were due to be picked up by friends the following day but luckily The Erewash Preservation and Development Association came to the rescue. Although I am underwhelmed by the Erewash Canal, it is due to the hard work of people of this association, and many similar others, that these canals have been saved from closure and not lost completely to unappreciative boaters like me.

So I was able to leave the boat securely locked in their basin for ten days. I paid £10 deposit for the key, put it on my key-ring and promptly lost all my keys.

On coming back to the basin ten days later I discovered the keys were missing and had to scale a wall to get in. Getting into my boat isn't difficult: I just need to lean heavily against the hatch cover and the feeble bolt gives way. Because the weather was forecast to be hot I'd taken all my herbs and salads off the roof of the boat and put them in the bath in shallow water. That was not a good idea. They were all water-logged and dead. If I'd left them out on the roof I'm sure some of the friendly and helpful members of the society would have been happy to water them for me.

We spent too much time getting back onto the boat and the D. H. Lawrence museum would have been closed, so that was another place I didn't manage to visit. I did have a walk around Langley Mill where the cast from the old coal mines have now been transformed into green hills. I did feel that I was heading north; the area had a different feel from the southern end of the Grand Union. The terraced houses are still redolent of mining villages, and in the Asda supermarket the vowels of the staff were flatter and the customers were fatter.

Back down the Erewash. At Sandicare I rambled around the outside of the old Springfield Mill. It is now converted into apartments but when it was built, in Victorian times, it was for lace-makers. Springfield Mill is a handsome, impressive building with its high arched windows, four towers and variety of red and yellow brick work. It seems difficult to imagine that such craftsmanship and materials were used to create this solid, beautiful building, only a little more than 100 years ago, to house a manufacturing industry.

Lining the canals there are so many of these old industrial buildings, many now restored and turned into apartments or craft, antique and cultural centres. But many more now lay derelict, or even seemingly derelict. I have often passed an old building with its intricate brickwork still intact but with buddleia growing out of the cracks and bars at the windows, thinking what a shame it is that this fine old shell of a building no longer has a commercial use then to see a solitary light in an upstairs window or to hear the sound of machinery or be enveloped in the smell of solvents. We have lost so much of our fine, industrial architecture it would be sad if we can't preserve what is left. The level of care and workmanship that went into the building of these factories and warehouses will never be repeated. Today we have fabricated buildings that are cheap and quick to erect and don't have any inherent beauty or any sense of longevity.

Sandiacre is only seven miles from Nottingham, a city historically famous for its lace-making. Meandering along the canal system, which was built as a commercial enterprise to link sites of industry to their customers or their supplies of raw materials, it is interesting to discover the industry which was associated with various towns or areas. Some pockets of that industry still remain, at other times it is only the redundant buildings, current street or place names, or pub names that are the reminders.

In Loughborough setting out to find, what I was told was an excellent market, I discovered a bell-makers' museum dedicated to the long history of the making of bells (obviously) in the town. Sadly the museum was closed so I never visited it, neither did I find the market. In Wolverton a long stretch of semi-derelict factory runs alongside the canal. It was once a fitting-out site for train carriages, the painting of a long train along the brick wall is a clue to its former use. In Hemel Hempstead the group of mills are the reminders of the paper-making industry. Further along there is still the smell of paint from the neglected building that passes to our left. In Northampton there are the remnants of shoe-making industry. In Leicester there are old buildings that housed the hosiery and wool-weaving trades. The slow glide along the canal system is an ideal place to absorb the feel of these historic buildings. Roads often bypass these backwaters of industry and cars travel too fast for the passengers to notice the detail that went into the construction. On the canal tall chimneys still stand amongst rubble. Chutes and cranes still overhang the water where once goods where lowered onto waiting barges. In the Fens redundant but restored pumping stations stand by the water's edge.

In Burton on Trent their industry of beer making is not a thing of the past. The whole town is still dedicated to the production of beers. The smell of hops and malt pervades the area. I understood it was the purity of the water that first brought the brewing industry here. I'm not sure if the Trent would be considered pure now; it certainly doesn't look it.

I'd stopped at Burton on Trent on my last trip along the Trent and Mersey and I enjoyed my rambles around the town, sniffing the air, looking at the large new factories that blew fragrant steam into the warm summer air. Interspersed were the older buildings of the brewing industry, some now apartments, some still producing beer in the new micro-breweries. The town centre was ordinary, with all the usual suspects in local parade of shops but I liked it. It was compact and homely. Maybe the sun was shining or maybe it was the effect of all the beer fumes that wafted around the town. The brewing industry in the town is dominated by Coors, even the Brewery Museum was labelled the Coors Visitors Centre. I was told that they have obliterated all mention of the Bass brewery and its logo, the distinctive red triangle. It is a logo that even I, a non-beer drinker, remembers.

I made a visit to the Marstons' brewery, one of the original brewers that still sit on the banks of the Trent. I found that it wasn't the waters of the Trent that gave the original Burton beers their distinctive flavour; it was water taken from wells that had passed through layers of rock that gave the water a high sulphur content. The Trent was only a help to the expansion of the brewing industry when it was made navigable in 1712 (the Trent and Mersey canal was built about 60 years later). It enabled the brewers to spread out.

From supplying only local customers they were able to send their ales abroad through the port at Hull.

I thoroughly enjoyed my trip around the brewery although my friend enjoyed it more because I don't like beer he got to drink my tasting samples as well as his own.

Coventry and Cathedrals

Coming off the Erewash Canal we turned left and onto the Trent. It was great to be on a wide, flowing river after the narrow, still confines of the canal. It felt like freedom. Freedom didn't last long: only as far as Nottingham when I'd decided to turn around and come back again. The need to fit in some work and the fact another grandchild was due, this time in London, suddenly made a journey into the frozen wastes of the north impractical. At Nottingham I managed a brief look around, bought a fridge and a hob at the marina and I went for a drink in the Ye Olde Trip to Jerusalem. Ye Olde Trip to Jerusalem is one of many 'oldest pubs in England' many of them called Ye Olde Something or other. It is built against the rock that Nottingham Castle stands on and with its warren of rooms it is atmospheric and probably does have the best Ye Olde name. After lingering too long in the pub there wasn't time for a visit to Nottingham Castle and, reluctantly, we turned and headed back south.

Then it was back onto the canal system at Shardlow, along the Trent and Mersey canal, turn left at Fazeley Junction onto the Coventry Canal. All routes I had travelled before but it still seemed a fresh journey, probably made fresher by my bad memory. As I couldn't remember where I'd been I saw many places as if for the first time; admittedly heading in the opposite direction and mooring at different places does make for variety. Diverse weather conditions made the walks I took and the way I spent my evenings different from the first journey. Warm and sunny: sit out on a towpath. Pouring with rain: dive into a pub. For whatever reason I was seeing the area as if in a new light.

I walked to Tamworth because photographs of it made it look interesting. Its Norman castle overlooks water meadows, and the market place was picturesque. Also, I'd never been there. As I crossed the water meadow I had a feeling of déjà vu. When I saw the block of flats that overlooks the town and remembered a café that was good and, more importantly, cheap I knew I'd wandered this way before. The town centre of Tamworth is pleasant with its statue of Robert Peel standing in front of the early eighteenth-century town hall and the castle that overlooks a park. The market square stands where it has stood for centuries it's just that damn block of flats that spoils it. High rise and ugly it peers down the High Street and seems to be in the eye-line at all times.

I definitely knew I'd never been to Coventry. Moored on the canal at Hawkesbury Junction we'd arranged to meet up with friends that evening for a meal at the lively, boaty pub the Greyhound. With a day to wait we decided to go down the lock-free Coventry Arm. Like many branch arms with an industrial purpose the Coventry Arm is more

271

functional than decorative. We were warned by a boater heading towards us that there was a submerged motor-bike under the next bridge and to keep to the left to avoid it. I kept to the left but the judder from the boat, the tilt to the left and the long scraping noise as we progressed under the bridge suggested that I hadn't quite avoided it.

The basin at the end of the Coventry, similar to the basins at Langley Mill and Market Harborough, is reminiscent of the original purpose of the canals. A statue of James Brindley peruses plans amidst the old buildings once used for canal maintenance and local industry. It is only a short walk into the centre of Coventry. I wanted to visit the cathedral, or rather the two cathedrals, for the old bombed out one sits next to the new one.

I was particularly interested in the new cathedral designed by Basil Spence in the 1950's, but I became enthralled by the old building, ruined and largely unrestored, as the German bombers had left it (although, no doubt a lot of tidying up had gone on afterwards). The cross from the charred roof trusses, that sat on an altar of rubble, was particularly emotive (even though I found out later that it was a copy, the original, symbolically put together the day after the bombing, was now on a staircase linking the old with the new). I was sorry I was short on time, for I could have spent hours poking around in corners, visiting crypts and reading notices.

The new cathedral is as stunning as the ruins of the old, although obviously in a different way. It was built in 1950's as a modern, iconic building. To me it had a feel of the fifties about it, rather than a feel of the futuristic. That in no way detracted from the impact of the building: the wall hanging by Graham Sutherland; the sculptures by Jacob Epstein and Elizabeth Frink; the magnificent multi-coloured window by John Piper. Yet maybe the most perfect sculpture in the new building is the old ruin as it is framed by the large, arched west screen that looks out onto it. To stand in front of the window and look at the blackened remains of the stone turrets and towers is moving. The only thing that spoils the carefully positioned view, from new cathedral to old, is a high-rise block of flats beyond them that stand defiantly in the eye-line poking one finger up at all this carefully planned architecture.

I had enjoyed my visits to the unpretentious cathedrals at Leicester and Birmingham, both havens of quiet in busy cities. They were once the parish churches and as the cities grew around them their status was upgraded. Maybe it was the growth of the cities rather than the magnificence of the buildings that demanded the title of cathedral yet both still had their charm and their history. And why do the impressive buildings of York and Beverley have the titles of minster rather than cathedral? Ely and Peterborough deserve their titles, soaring and substantial, and at the same time quiet and contemplative. Ely especially, high on a hill overlooking the flat Fens, is an incredible feat of medieval building, its power visible for miles around.

To extend my list of cathedral visiting I had hopped on a bus at Hopwas to travel to Lichfield. Lichfield Cathedral is famously touted as being the only one in this country with three spires. I stood in front of it and wondered if this was Lichfield's only claim to fame, I think I'd have preferred one high, impressive spire to these three chunky, ornate brown stone ones. I thought all of the dark brown stone building resembled St. Pancras station, only with more statues. But St. Pancras is mock gothic, Lichfield is the real thing. Once inside Lichfield Cathedral I fell in love with it. It almost replaced Ely in my affections. There is an intense sense of the past inside this beautiful building with its stained glass and wall hangings and the tattered flags captured by the Staffordshire Regiment. There are many stone statues and ornately carved tombs of the great and the good from throughout the history of Lichfield yet it was the smaller carvings I became absorbed with. Along the wall of the aisle are the small heads carved from stone, probably replacing originals destroyed by Oliver Cromwell's troops during the Civil War. These aren't the heads of the bishops, dignitaries and fearless soldiers but the faces of the ordinary people of Lichfield. This is the face of the old woman in the mobcap; these of the bearded dandy, the farmer and the young girl. This woman sold eggs in the market place, that man spent too long in the taverns. You could imagine each and every one of them strolling through Lichfield on market day all those centuries ago.

I am not religious but I do love the cathedrals and churches that I get the chance to visit when I'm roaming around the rivers and canals. There is a sense of peace in these places; maybe the centuries of contemplation of worshippers has permeated the ancient stone-work. Most

274

churches are locked during the day and I can only manage to peer through windows or poke around the churchyard. Although the churchyards themselves are worth a visit with their fallen angels and family tombs, some graves cared for many years after the incumbent died, others rapidly neglected. The gravestones give an indication of local names, the tombs of local dignitaries, sometimes the headstones sadly mark the fate of brothers who fought and died in the First World War. Even hundreds of years later the graves of children have a poignancy, especially when they list siblings who all died in infancy.

Sometimes I have been lucky to find a solitary, country church open. I sat quietly for an hour watching as the faded red, blues and greens of a medieval wall painting emerged from beneath their covering of white plaster, as a restorer, perched on a scaffold, patiently worked. At St. Helen's in Abingdon I met a very informative man who gave me the story of their incredible, fourteenth century roof panels that made up the Tree of Jesse (the family tree of Jesus, a fact I wouldn't have known without my guide). Walking up the hill from the Thames I was able to sit in a church as the light faded from the stained-glass windows. By the time the churchwarden came to lock up, making the heavy wooden door boom shut behind us and the large iron key grate in the lock, the birds in the graveyard had ceased their chatter and a fine, dusky mist was settling in the valley obliterating all sights and sounds. It was a scene that traversed the centuries.

At the ornate 17th century All Saints Church in the centre of Northampton the delight was the transcript of the poem 'I am' by John Clare which they claimed was composed on the steps of their church. As the smell of chips wafted through from the café in the entrance and the bustle of a town carried on outside, I stood and read it. It is a concise and disturbing poem written by a man dealing with mental illness, some reports say it was written while he was in Northampton Asylum. Probably the poem is as relevant today to some of the rough sleepers of Northampton, as it was nearly four hundred years ago to John Clare.

Yet often it is the redundant churches that are the most memorable. Stripped of the bibles and hassocks, notices of services and mother's union meetings, bereft of flowers and church paraphernalia, the view of the workmanship of the original builders and stonemasons is uninterrupted. In their emptiness they are tranquil, evocative of their time and of the purpose for which they were built.

I Am!

BY JOHN CLARE (1844)

I am—yet what I am none cares or knows;
My friends forsake me like a memory lost:
I am the self-consumer of my woes—
They rise and vanish in oblivious host,
Like shadows in love's frenzied stifled throes
And yet I am, and live—like vapours tossed

Into the nothingness of scorn and noise,
Into the living sea of waking dreams,
Where there is neither sense of life or joys,
But the vast shipwreck of my life's esteems;
Even the dearest that I loved the best
Are strange—nay, rather, stranger than the rest.

I long for scenes where man hath never trod
A place where woman never smiled or wept
There to abide with my Creator, God,
And sleep as I in childhood sweetly slept,
Untroubling and untroubled where I lie
The grass below—above the vaulted sky.

Towards Stratford-upon-Avon

I stopped at Braunston to get a new cratch cover fitted. When I first bought the boat I hated the cratch cover. It made the inside dark, it made sitting in the sharp end of the bow uncomfortable and it made climbing into the boat more awkward. It was going to go. Then winter came and it helped stop the draughts and it made a dry area for wood and coal and even in winter on a sunny day it was warm and sheltered enough to enable me to sit out with my morning coffee. It was going to stay. When it acquired more patches than original material and the zips finally gave up the ghost I was happy to replace it. Although to say I was happy was maybe a bit of a stretch for I had to cough up hundreds of pounds.

Once the fitting was done and my sister was on board we were off back along the Oxford and heading towards Warwick, planning on journeying to Stratford-upon-Avon. The first part of the journey was easy. A pootle along the Grand Union in fine sunny weather, turn right at Napton Junction and through the three Calcutt Locks. There we met up with a father and daughter who were taking a boat to the Saltisford Arm and we had an efficient and amiable passage up the locks together. They were travelling on up the

Stockton Flight; we were undecided as to whether or not go with them as they were easy travelling companions but it was getting late in the afternoon and we decided to call it a day when we neared the top of the flight. That was a mistake. The following day dawned grey and gloomy and heavy rain was forecast for later in the morning. As we were meeting family the next day in Long Itchington we thought we'd set out early to beat the rain but the rain arrived sooner than forecast and beat us to the locks. It poured down. All locks were against us. The family we paired up with were complete novices and had to spend more time stopping their children from falling in the canal than operating the locks. I was wet. Marcelle operating the locks was even wetter. She was cold, fed-up of me just standing there issuing instructions and exhausted by the heavy gates and stiff paddles. She managed nine locks, refused to do the tenth, had a hot shower and went to bed for the rest of the day. We did the last lock the next morning and met up with our family.

For the next two days the locks were widely spaced and we didn't hurry, stopping and looking, drinking and eating. We had a long day in the lovely Regency town of Leamington Spa, then a visit to Warwick and the fascinating Lord Leycester Hospital. I think the 14th century building is made even more fascinating because it is still used for the purpose it was originally created, a place of retirement for old soldiers. Our tour of the building was conducted by one of the residents, known as the Brethren, and was both informative and entertaining.

Then the Hatton flight was ahead of us. If the ten locks at Stockton had almost defeated Marcelle, I wasn't sure what the twenty-one locks at Hatton would do to her so I phoned Bob and asked if he fancied a couple of days on a boat. Never one to refuse a bit of boating he came to join us. We met up with an older couple for the first two Cape Locks but she had hurt her back and couldn't do the locks and wouldn't drive the boat. It meant the husband drove the boat and expected us three to do all the work, including tying him up and letting the water in very slowly so it didn't rattle him about. We decided to stop for an early lunch and let them go on ahead. We set off again an hour later and caught them up at the next lock. In circumstances like that I'm inclined to mutter into my boots, and grumble away behind their backs and then get on with doing the locks myself. Bob is more forthright. He told the reluctant lady that she had to do her bit. He said that if somebody as ditsy as her (pointing to me) could drive a boat so could she. I think she was more scared of Bob than of handling a fifty-foot boat because she did as she was told and after a couple of nervous entries into the first two locks she became quite confident and chatty. Bob did something similar on the Buckby Flight to an American couple travelling with their granddaughter. Fed-up of working the first two locks alone when two women were sitting inside playing on their phones, he tapped on the window and told them to get out and help. Again a bad back meant no lock wheeling from the woman; she had to stay nervously in the lock with the boat, while her husband opened the paddles and gates. However, Bob wasn't ferocious enough to scare the lumpen granddaughter into action. She just remained where she was, inside and glued to her i-phone.

Bob wasn't much kinder to Marcelle. When she was struggling with a heavy gate and asked for help all his response was 'you women asked for equality so don't complain when you get it.' Then he went back to trying to light his cigarette in the wind and left her to it.

Hatton Flight done we went up the Grand Union and turned left onto the Stratford Canal. After first taking advantage of his car to visit some more of the area we sent Bob home.

We joined the Stratford-upon-Avon Canal at the Lapworth link. It was a pleasant stroll back along the Lapworth Flight secure in the knowledge that we wouldn't be doing these nineteen locks; we were turning left and there were only the three remaining locks of the flight ahead of us. We didn't make it as far as Stratford-upon-Avon. We enjoyed the Stratford Canal too much; we dawdled and explored, we took too long at the locks, we were held up by boats going slowly ahead of us, we tied up and took too long over lunch. At Wootton Wawen (should it really be Wootton Warren but was named by a short-tongued inhabitant) we wandered around the village with its timbered houses and then thought the tea room looked tempting so that was that day gone. By the time we reached Wilmcote we realised we weren't going to get to Stratford and instead spent the day in at Mary Arden's House and Farm. Marcelle, of course, denied that the thought of the eleven locks of the Wimlcote flight in any way influenced her decision to tarry too long in Wilmcote village.

Each canal has its own identity, the locks may all be painted black and white but the mechanisms vary. Feeds from rivers giving clear flowing water; collapsed salt workings making wide lakes; winding contour canals; dead straight uninteresting canals. A feature of the Stratford is the old iron bridges with a split in the centre which enabled the towing rope to be pulled through, and the charming bell roofed lock-keepers' cottages that line the canal. Many of them are now holiday cottages. At Lowsonford Lock I slowly rose from the depths to see two women sitting in the window of the cottage, laughing and raising glasses of wine to me. I suppose it must be amusing to see the top of the head emerging gradually, slowly followed by the rest of the person and then, eventually, the boat appearing. On the other side of the lock yet another Anthony Gormley statue peered down, watching me emerging. At least this statue was more representational and less realistic so at least I didn't have to eyeball his private parts as I gradually rose.

Something else the Stratford has is an aqueduct: quite a long high aqueduct really. I'm used to heading towards an aqueduct that is marked on the map, blinking and not noticing it. I didn't miss this one; it is impressive. I would have enjoyed the view if it wasn't for my fear of heights. I looked down and my stomach churned. Marcelle, sitting in the bow with her book came back to the stern and announced 'that was a bit scary.'

Back at the Lapworth Link Bob arrived, took Marcelle to the station for her to get the train to the airport and we turned went back the way we'd come. Bob likes cruising, he doesn't believe in stopping so the journey that had taken us five days on the way out took us about six hours on the way back. In no time we were back at Long Itchington and visiting the Two Boats pub.

The one strange thing about stopping near the pub this time and the subsequent trip down the Thames was that we timed it right for entertainment. Usually the brilliant band was on last week, the quiz night is tomorrow, we stop on the only day of the week that the interesting museum is closed or the event we wanted to visit is rained off. This time when we pulled up we noticed that that night there was a pub quiz and the following night a performance by the Mikron Theatre, a company which tours by canal boat.

We should have known the pub quiz was a serious event when we saw the car park was full and all the tables were taken by teams of six players. We squeezed onto a table in the corner. On one round we couldn't even understand the questions so we weren't surprised to win the booby price. In fact, we were quite pleased to win the booby prize when I calculated the value of the packs of seeds we had won and estimated that it was actually worth more per person than the cash prize for winning that was shared by two teams of six.

The following night there was a production, outside the pub, celebrating 100 years of the WI. It rained. The players were dry under their canopied stage. The audience weren't. The standers at the back persuaded the sitters at the front to put down their umbrellas and join the rest of us in a soaking and allow all of us to see the stage. Then it didn't seem to matter that the rain was sluicing down. It wasn't cold rain and boaters have wet weather gear and somehow it added to the atmosphere of the evening. After all we're British; soggy BBQs, wet weddings, drenched theatrical performances are all part of our heritage. It helped that the performance was excellent. Maybe if it had been tedious the rain dripping down the back of my neck would have sent me into the bar instead of standing outside watching.

Once More Onto The Thames

Onto the lovely, lovely Thames using the not-so-lovely Dukes Cut to get from the Oxford Canal to the Thames. We stopped this time on the river in Oxford below Osney Bridge. In the pub that was stepping distance from the boat there were a group of musicians playing Irish music. I love Irish music and was happy to stand and tap my foot for the rest of the evening. Bob, after the first hour said it was too repetitive and went back to the boat leaving me still happily jigging about and drinking cider.

All of the Thames was as I remembered. This was not surprising as I doubt the atmosphere and the environment of the river has changed much in a hundred years, much less in two years. Okay so there is more development around the towns especially downriver, than there was a century ago. The cruisers are bigger and motorised and there are fewer skiffs and rowing-boats than in previous less mechanised years but the locks have changed little and the water meadows, the wide reaches and the islands and back waters retain the same idyllic atmosphere that so many writers have enthused about.

Progress was intentionally slow; the next day we only got as far as Abingdon. The following day we stopped for lunch just outside Wallingford and moored against a steep bank-side. Music drifted over the water from the town. I said I would go and investigate and scrambled up the bank only to come face to face with a hulking herd of bullocks. I scrambled back onto the boat, ate my lunch and we went on our way. Later moored at Beale's Park, still curious about the music at Wallingford I Googled it and found we had just sailed past the Wallingford Bunkfest. The next morning we turned around and went back. The mooring amongst the bullocks was taken so we went under the bridge passed the town and lassoed a couple of trees on a mooring that wasn't really a mooring. Access to dry land was a crawl off the stern, trying not to skewer eyeballs on the blackthorn bushes, trying to avoid the patches of nettles and then hauling our unfit bodies up the steep bank. Getting back was easier, just a skid and slide down the steep bank and land with a bump on the stern canopy.

It was worth the effort of turning back. Wallingford Bunkfest was brilliant. A weekend of diverse music in the pubs, streets and on the main stage. For the last few weeks we seemed to have been in the right place at the right time for entertainment. Long may it last.

At Hampton Court our entertainment was a celebration for the new commodore of a nearby boater's club. Boat after boat went past, all smart white expensive cruisers, including some tall very, very expensive cruisers. There were no tatty old narrowboats belonging to these boat club members. The crews, blue blazered and white hatted stood to attention and saluted the new commodore as they went past his moored boat. Occasionally the salute was over-exaggerated and ironic, mostly the salutes would not have shamed the crew of a war-ship piping an admiral on board. I was moored next to the elegant cruiser with the new commodore on board. I tried a few salutes, waves and general acrobatics with fingers and hands in the general direction of the flotilla of passing boats but got no response whatsoever. I thought of suggesting a similar ceremony for the new commodore of our much less salubrious boat club on the River Nene. But that wouldn't work, the members probably only own one smart blazer between them and telling them to sail past and salute the new commodore would only be asking for trouble.

The diversity of boats and boaters on the Thames is one of the joys of being on this river. I have possibly shared locks with these tall cruisers and their champagne sipping crews and have always had friendly smiles and polite conversations. There are plenty of stories of owners of expensive vessels being sniffy or downright rude about the hoi-polloi tucked into the lock below them but personally I have never experienced it.

It was great being able to moor here next to the incredible Hampton Court Palace, a place I have visited often but never tire of. We did visit and spent hours wandering around the state rooms, the kitchens and gardens. I still had *Three Men in a Boat* and reread the chapter whea they got hopelessly lost in the maze. Bob and I weren't going to do

287

that, finding the way around a maze is easy. We separated at the entrance and said 'last one to the centre buys the drinks.' Neither of us made it to the centre, we bumped into each other a few times and then went our separate ways again. Rather like the three men, who had many followers by the time darkness fell, I acquired a young Indian couple and their mother and we all got lost together. In the end when we all neared an exit rather than the centre we gave up and went to the tea-rooms. I wonder how many times over the last century the scenario set by Jerome K Jerome, of getting lost in Hampton Court Maze, has been re-created.

This time I was planning on going on down the Thames, by-passing the delights of the Slug and Lettuce at Staines, through the lock at Teddington and then turn left onto the Grand Union at Brentford. The stretch of the Thames from Teddington to Brentford is tidal and boats are only allowed through the huge Teddington lock two hours either side of high water.

I find that there is a sense of adventure engendered by mooring up and waiting for a tide to change. Of giving details of travel to the lock-keepers, of speaking to other boaters about the problems that could be encountered (but rarely are) on this stretch of water. There is a sense of anticipation when the high-water time approaches and the first batch of boats, the ones going on the tideway up to Limehouse and beyond, are slotted into the lock ready to be let out onto the tidal waters. Then it's our turn. The lock-keepers fit the boats together as one would a jig-saw puzzle, my guide book says that I should have VHF radio (which I haven't) but nobody checks that I possess one and know how to use it. There are ten boats in the lock, a motley collection of small and large cruisers, new and old narrow-boats. Most of us are heading onto the canal system at Brentford, some of the cruisers are heading further downriver.

Positioned as directed we wait, ropes held, the water comes into the lock, the gates open and we're off. We're towards the back of the lock and one of the last out. The cruisers steam away into the distance, sunlight glinting on their white bows the rest of us spread out, there is so much room on this wide river and nothing coming towards; none of the canoes, rowing boats, sailing boats or skiffs which had made the last few miles of travel on the Thames interesting. Interesting because of the risk of squashing boats and their occupants. Interesting because unpredictable sailing boats turned suddenly under the bows, canoeists decided to stop for a rest in the path of the boat or a swimmer appeared from nowhere, suddenly in range of the propeller. Concentration and a steady hand were needed.

Now we were free to just go our own pace, we passed a couple of narrow-boats chugging along and settled down to admire the scenery. Passed Eel Pie Island, the place made legendary in the sixties for hedonism and music by the likes of the Stones, the Kinks and Bowie. On the opposite bank there is Ham House, always an elegant mansion, never known as a site of sex drugs and rock and roll as was its less illustrious neighbour across the river. Passed Teddington and onwards to where the hills of Richmond rise above the river, framing its Georgian buildings, its pubs and riverside walks.

Trip boats wait for customers, rowing boats and cruisers are moored along the bankside. Oh, look there's the pub I used to go to. I remember having to paddle back to the car when a high tide was very high.

Into the canal entrance at Brentford. In discussions with other boaters we had been warned the entrance could be tricky and it would be best to go past the turning, do a 180 degree turn and come back in against the tide. That is what the two narrowboats ahead of us did but the tide was slack and Bob, who was driving, decided just to sweep in. That worked perfectly and we seemed to sneak in, out of turn, ahead of one of the boats that travelled further downstream before turning. The intention wasn't to grab his place in the lock so when we got blasts on the horn and shaken fists from him we just suggested he went on ahead, which he did, still scowling at us.

The Thames to Teddington is under the jurisdiction of the Environment Agency. Once on the tidal section it becomes part of the Port of London Authority. Turning into the lock at Brentford we are back under the jurisdiction and licencing requirements of the Canal & River Trust. Back on the canal system: narrow, still, murky water; litter and over-hanging trees. I wanted to turn back and go up the beautiful, fascinating Thames again.

Another Winter!

It was autumn. Autumn was still in its guise of 'mists and mellow fruitfulness.' The days were shorter but they were still mild and although the nights were longer and chillier, the fire didn't have to be lit until late in the evening. I was still in London so even dark evenings were populated and lively and there wasn't the same sense of impending winter that there is in rural locations. My vague plan was to head down the Lee Canal for the winter and see if the marinas at Hertford or Stansted Abbots, had a winter mooring slot. I may have left it a bit late as I'd already called two marinas on the Stort and they didn't have any spaces. But as the weather was still clement I wasn't too bothered about there being no room at the inn I'd just do the continuous cruising again. I was still in optimistic mode and I'd decided to forget how much I hate the darkness of winter when I am moored in a quiet place.

I was gradually making my way towards Hertford and was at the lock on the west side of Victoria Park just before I was due to make the sharp left turn onto the Hertford Canal. It was difficult to tie up because there was a dirty, white, wide-beam boat moored alongside the lock landing. If my memory was correct the same boat was moored there when I came past months ago. I tied up next to him and scrambled over the boat hoping to leave dirty footprints on the deck although, as the deck was covered in windblown leaves and crisp packets, I didn't think a few muddy footprints would make much difference. Feeling grumpy about boats moored in places that caused me inconvenience I stomped over to the lock gates to open the paddles and empty the lock. I'd had just put my windlass in the downstream gate mechanism when a C&RT volunteer emerged from the building on the left and crossed over the lock gate to help me. As the water gushed through the paddles we leant on the gates and chatted about nothing in particular. I asked why the dirty white boat was still on the lock landing and he said it had supposedly broken down and that there was little the authorities could do about getting it moved.

When the lock was almost empty, the volunteer said, 'I'll open the gate. You go and get your boat.' I headed off in one direction and he headed off in the other direction to open the bottom gate.

'Why are you going that way?' he asked me.

'To get my boat,' I told him.

We both looked down at the empty lock and then towards my boat tied up against the wide-beam and realisation dawned that I had just emptied a lock that was in my favour. All I had needed to do was open a gate and drive in. We went to the upstream gates in silence and wound the paddles up to re-fill the lock.

The volunteer on duty at the lock did tell me that the Hertford canal was going to be closed in the next few days and would be closed for at least three weeks so that repairs could be made to the locks. When I turned into the canal I could see there were quite a few spare mooring places, which is unusual in this part of the London canal where boats are usually double parked. I thought, it must be quiet because the canal was going to be closed and boaters didn't want to be trapped there without any facilities. The C&RT have a winter schedule for lock closures. Winter boaters who are on the move carefully plan their journeys so they don't get trapped between locks for weeks or months on end. Other boaters who don't want to be moving far stock up with fuel and water and make sure their sewage systems are empty so they are able to stay put. Then because of the closures on the canal they do not have the hassle of enforcement officers moving them on. I made a quick calculation about my movements and plans for the next few weeks, decided that I fell into the latter category and a three-week, or maybe more, lock-in at Victoria Park would suit me fine. I'd got a full water tank and an empty toilet system and had places to go and people to see. Winter was approaching. I didn't want to be moving too far. I pushed to the back of my mind that I would be walking back to my boat on dark nights at the edge of a park where a jogger was brutally murdered one morning and another sexually assaulted. It was on the other side of Victoria Park that my daughter was mugged one evening when she was flat hunting. But on a bright autumn morning when burnished leaves carpeted the towpath it looked pleasant and peaceful, an oasis of tranquillity in the busy East End of London. I tied up and settled down.

At lunch-time I went out on a sortie of the area and headed towards the Roman Road market. It's a great place, a typical London street market, with cheap clothing and dodgy electrical stalls, amazing fruit and veg and a vibrant atmosphere. I went into a traditional London Pie and Mash shop and forgoing the chance to try jellied eels, I bought a steak pie, mash and liquor to take back to the boat. I was sitting on the boat enjoying the pie and mash (not so sure about the liquor which is a thin parsley sauce) when there was a knock on the roof. It was a man from C&RT.

'Do you know the canal will be closed from Monday for repairs to the lock?'

'Yes, I had heard but it's okay I don't mind if I get trapped here for a few weeks.'

'Well did you know that to repair the locks the canal is going to be drained?'

'Aaaah no. So that explains why there are few boats moored along here.'

He admonished me for not reading the many notices pinned along the railings. When his lecture was over he got on his bike and pedalled away. I finished my pie and mash and gave myself a talking to about the need to be more observant. That was the second time in a few hours that I failed to notice the obvious. Then I untied and moved on. I headed in the direction of Hackney, luckily setting off just in time to meet up with a nice young man on a blue boat who as going in my direction which meant I had help through the awkward locks.

Then it was on to the Lee Canal where the boats were, once again, double moored, the usual crowding around here was probably exacerbated by closure of the Hertford arm. I reached the Middlesex filter beds before I saw a suitable space where I could moor alongside a sixty-foot boat that would give me access across its stern. Not being the most agile of boaters when tying up against another boat I must make sure that I can get on and off without having to do feats of athleticism along gunwales, and leaps across bows or roofs. The protocol when tying up alongside a boat is to ask if is okay. There was nobody on board this boat and on this crowded stretch of canal if boaters object to having other boats tied up alongside them it's tough. They should moor up in the middle of the countryside not next to Hackney Marshes.

When the boat's resident, a young woman, returned from work on her bike, she was happy for me to be snuggled up against her, helped me retie the ropes onto her boat and told me that as the enforcement officer had visited that morning and only came by twice a week we will be good to stay here for more than the allotted fourteen days.

Just The One Shaggy Dog Story

All boating books seem to include tales about their endearing on-board dogs. This is my only story about the slightly less than endearing dog that found its way to my boat. After this I promise there will be no mention of dogs.

By the time it came to leave the mooring by the filter beds the young woman on the inside of me had moved off and I'd taken her place against the towpath. Another boat had tied up against me. Bob and his dog Max had joined me to head off up the Lee Canal. When we wanted to move away we had to untie the boat, reverse out and then re-moor our neighbour alongside the towpath. It wasn't a complicated manoeuvre for two people but it was a time consuming one that needed concentration. Untangled from the other boat we sailed away, passed through the lock at Lea Bridge and then stopped about two miles further along the canal at Tottenham Hale to do some shopping for food. Then the question was asked, 'Where's the dog?'

       'He's in the kitchen with you.'

       'No he's not. I thought he was on the stern with you.'

It turned out we had left the dog behind and it was up to me to go back and look for him (Bob's knee was suddenly hurting). I picked up the lead and started walking back. About half a mile from the filter beds I rounded a bend and in front of me was Max. He took one look at me, turned tail and fled at full pelt in the opposite direction. I was puzzled; maybe it wasn't Max, maybe it was just a Max look alike. So, I carried on walking. I reached the point at which we had been moored and there was Max sitting patiently, like a good dog should, waiting for our return. The image of a good dog was rather ruined because he was still muddy, sweaty and panting from his headlong dash back from where he'd seen me to where he'd been left.

Why did he do that? Don't ask me. I don't understand dogs. I don't understand men either. Give me cats and women any day.

Called Away

I moored up at Waltham Forest. I did some work in London and then went to stay with a friend. In the time I was away from the boat the clocks had gone back, gale force winds had denuded the trees of their remaining leaves and heavy rain had turned the towpath into a quagmire. I'd left the boat on a gentle autumn day and returned to a winter's day of squally showers and bleakness. The boat felt cold and damp and the fridge, and more importantly the wine rack, were empty. I hadn't even got my coat off when the phone rang and my son-in-law told me my daughter had been taken to hospital. I rapidly picked up my unpacked bag and left.

She was in hospital for over a week and needed help with her ten-week old baby when she was released so I obviously wasn't going anywhere on the boat for a few weeks. I rang C&RT and explained the situation and, as on previous occasions when I asked for leeway, they were sympathetic and helpful. The movements of boats are monitored thoroughly now. In the past twelve months I had been clocked by enforcement officers on the Erewash Canal, in Nottingham, in Coventry, in Braunston and all points south so they only had to look at my details to know that I really was continuously cruising. I may have stretched some of the staying times a little, especially in the previous winter but I'd only had two, polite, requests to move on. One when I was at the seven-day mooring at Kensal Green. I received an email from C&RT saying that I had been recorded as been two days over the specified mooring time. By the time I received the email I had left Kensal Green. I replied telling them I'd moved now but that I'd stayed on because I wasn't feeling well and it was cold and wet outside. They responded with 'Happy New Year and we hope you feel better soon.' A response I thought was rather sweet and proved there were people at the end of the line and not just automated responses. When the enforcement officer recorded me as an over-stayer at Croxley I had just moved off the mooring and was heading away down the canal. I thought it was rather too zealous of him to then report me but I suppose there was nothing to prove I hadn't seen him coming along the towpath and just decided to hover mid-canal until he passed by. In Ely where the 48-hour stay was strictly monitored by traffic wardens it was known that they did their rounds between 8.30am and 9.30am and the regulars in that area would take a brief trip downriver or go to the waterpoint and then return in the hopes that nobody had sneaked into their space in the hour that they'd been away to avoid been monitored.

I came back to the boat in late December and moved it to Broxbourne. Then it was Christmas and the New Year and I was away. After that it didn't seem worthwhile putting the boat in a marina. I moved it gradually intending to stop at

Hertford but never got any further than Ware. There were some chilly journeys but also days of bright sunshine when it was a joy to be out. Somehow, with the help of the bolt hole of Bob's place, the winter ground past quite painlessly.

Feet

I have turned around and I am heading back towards London. I'm moored on the River Lea, or maybe I'm on the Lee Canal, next to Milford Park. The River Lea and the Lee Canal seem to be inter-changeable along its length from Limehouse to Hertford. I'm not sure why the Lea as a river is spelled Lee when it's a canal and a bit of half-hearted research on the internet doesn't come up with an explanation for the change of spelling.

Although my map doesn't tell me which length is canal and which is river I think, here at Lea Bridge, I'm now on the river. The banks are a canal-like concrete but the water is wide with a sharp bend that is more indicative of a river. Just beyond Lea Bridge opposite the Princess of Wales pub the water tumbles over a large weir and heads towards Old Ford. It used to feed the Middlesex filter beds which in Victorian times provided clean drinking water to East London. They are now dry and the water of a more populous London is dealt with by the large reservoirs which line the eastern banks of the river and have sophisticated water filtration units. They don't rely on the sand and gravel which was used to purify the water in Victorian times. The old filter beds are now part of a nature reserve and although the pumping stations have been removed, the outlines of the workings and the circular filter beds still remain. They provide a sculptural interest with straight blocks of stone which funnelled the water from the river and the round filter beds where the water was filtered through the sand and gravel and pumped to homes in East London. The remains of these one-hundred-and-fifty-year-old workings now nestle amongst reeds and wetland flowers. The old iron sluices and sand hoppers remain and sculptures have been formed from concrete blocks. The stones and blocks covered in lichen, the reeds and flowers, the birds and insects create a peaceful haven so close to the busy roads and give the impression of an ancient monument, yet it was only in the late 1960's, a little over one hundred years after their construction, that these workings were dismantled.

As the river flows over the weir, by-passing the filter beds and heads off east the navigable route once more becomes a canal, the Hackney Cut, which goes past the Olympic Park through densely populated London and down to the Thames.

The concrete bank here is very high and I have a long step down onto the gunwales to get back onto the boat. My short legs can just about manage the step down although I am tempted to sit down on the pathway, shuffle on my bum to the edge of the bank and lower myself onto the boat. If there was nobody watching I might take that undignified route, but here in busy E5 it is rare that there is nobody watching. So I drop

302

my bag and any shopping onto the cushions in the bow, grasp the running rail and cautiously step, a stretched leg at a time, onto my boat.

When I stand at my kitchen sink and look out of the window all I can see is the concrete bank topped by feet or by bicycle wheels, or pram wheels followed by feet, often feet and paws and sometimes the little wheels of a scooter with small feet vigorously propelling it along. The view may be limited but it is never boring. We rarely study feet. Faces, eyes, hair, retreating bums maybe but we don't often give feet more than a passing glance. Yet the saying 'well shod' and the insistence of my father that I would be judged by the condition of my shoes when I went for a job interview (advice that I ignored and may be why I didn't get many of jobs I was interviewed for, that and the fact I was always under qualified) suggests that feet and footwear are important. There is a fascination about passing feet and the way they are shod and there is also the bonus of not having to smile and nod every few minutes to people peering in the window. Feet are not interested in looking in narrowboats, although occasionally a child bends down to peer in but the sight of a strange woman standing there pulling faces at them soon cures them of that habit. They rapidly spring upright and cling to their mother.

I stand and watch the feet going past. Amongst the flashing wheels of bikes or the steady wheels of prams and pushchairs are the feet of the walkers, the joggers, the shufflers, the dog walkers, the dawdlers. In the morning black shod, office feet march briskly, going to my left. In the evening they return at a more leisurely pace. Mostly I have no curiosity about the person above the foot and ankle; a white trainer, an orange running shoe, a black casual slip-on, a leather brogue all quickly become commonplace. Occasionally the shoe is so bright or bizarre or so well-polished and obviously expensive that I have to squat down to see who is wearing such footwear. When trainers topped with jeans walk past I start my own competition of 'guess the gender.' I'm more often wrong than right, and sometimes even nipping to the front of the boat to get a better look as the wearer retreats doesn't answer the question. An inordinate number of people wearing trainers and jeans also seem to wear hoodies with the hood turned up.

I become mesmerized by the parade of feet each pair working to its own rhythm. Orange, lime green and pink running shoes flash past, plain running shoes with snazzy laces jog on by. A splash of colour, a glimpse of a well-turned ankle and they are gone. Down at heel, slip-on black shoes shuffle past slowly; small children's feet dance past. Smart black shoes march determinedly and stilettos totter. Women in full hijab seem to prefer white trainers, dog walkers prefer casual slip-ons. A pair of odd shoes passes by. I worked with a man who wore odd shoes as a fashion statement. These shoes of East London aren't a fashion statement they are simply a statement of homelessness and poverty.

I observe two pairs of feet hovering around outside the boat then moving away to examine the shrubbery that lines the tow-path. They definitely look like police feet. I bend down to look and confirm that the police feet are attached to policemen. My curiosity is awakened and I climb onto the gunwales to see what they are doing.

'Have you seen a tall young man in a blue sweater running past here?' They ask me.

'What shoes was he wearing?' I ask them.

They both give me a strange look. It transpires that they are looking in the shrubbery for heroin. There has just been a big drugs raid in the flats along the side of the park. One of the dealers did a runner and they suspect that he threw away his stash of heroin as he ran.

The man from the boat behind me has joined us and we are asked to look out for the packets of heroin. They look like lollipops we're told, only without the sticks and wrapped in shiny black, orange and blue packets.

When the police have moved on, the bloke from the boat behind and I are joined by the bloke from the boat in front of me. The three of us poke around in the shrubbery but only find some empty crisp packets and two syringes. We discuss what to do with the heroin if we find any: call the police or put it on ebay. The ebay option seems to be more lucrative and attractive even if it is illegal, so we all decide to go with ebay, but our decision is not put to the test as we don't find any heroin.

We lounge back against my boat and get to discussing crime and mishaps on the canal system. 'My mate found a torso wrapped in a bin bag under his boat recently,' said the man from the boat in front of me. 'And another mate found a body of an alchi in the lock by Victoria Park.'

'I had a dead Italian art thief behind my boat a few months ago,' said the man from the boat behind me. 'I was moored at the mouth of the Islington Tunnel. I came home from work and the police were crawling over my boat and dragging the body out. He was attached to a Tesco's shopping trolley. My boat features quite clearly in the photos that were published in the national press.'

Wow... For tales of dead bodies under the boat or in the canal finding the body of an Italian art thief takes some beating. It's not just your usual drunk in the canal or even a gangland murder or drugs related retribution killing; an Italian art thief is real international crime. Although I'm more impressed that he was found attached to a Tesco's trolley. I know that pushing shopping trolleys into the canal is an urban sport but they don't usually have bodies attached to them. I comment that pushing a trolley all the way from Tesco to the mouth of the Islington Tunnel with a body on board must have been quite a feat of steering; I find it difficult to safely negotiate the baked beans aisle with most of their trollies.

The man from the boat in front points out that they probably just fished the trolley out of the canal and then tied the first available dead body to it. I suppose in the absence of useful blocks of concrete this would be the most practical and likely scenario, but I still prefer the image of a gang of sharply dressed art dealers pushing a wonky Tesco's trolley, complete with a dead body, through the affluent streets of Islington.

I can't compete in these tales of dead body one-upmanship. I've only had a dead dog under my boat. I

306

smelled dreadful but wasn't a traumatic find and it certainly didn't make it into the national press. There is no sign of the jettisoned heroin and we two boaters can't cap the third boater's tale of the dead Italian art thief so all three of us drift back to our boats.

I make a cup of coffee and stand in the bow drinking it. In the park across the towpath a muscled young man does hand-stands on a parallel bar, one of the pieces of equipment that the park provides in the hope of improving the fitness of local residents. In contrast, beyond him, two yellow-jacketed medics are dealing with an elderly man slumped under a tree. The two policemen are now heading back towards the block of flats where the lights of the police van are still pulsating, repeatedly reflecting shades of blue on the white wall of the building. On Lea Bridge Road the rush hour traffic is at a standstill and a cacophony of horns and sirens sound.

It's just another day in East London.

Leaving London

The canals and waterways of London were always crammed with boats but they seem even fuller now than they were two years ago when I first cruised along here. All the boats are double parked, mooring spaces are impossible to find. I end up moving for far longer each day than I intended to, or alternatively stopping after an hour because I spot a space. Despite the number of boats in the London area, water and disposal facilities are few and far between so either planning is necessary or if a water point is spotted there is a quick stop to fill the tank. Most of the additional boats are live-aboards often these are young people trying to find an alternative to the horrendous price of renting or buying accommodation in London. The average age of boaters on the Grand Union Canal must be in the sixties. In London the average age is much, much younger. Mostly they are registered as continuous cruisers because the price of a fixed mooring in this area is also horrendous. Rumour has it that the regulars are in contact with each other and their moving is synchronised so that they move into each other's spaces when they reach the end of their fourteen-day stay. All this annoys leisure boaters who want to spend a few weeks in London before passing through to Hertford or Bishops Stortford. There must be a solution but I'm not sure what it is. Paid visitor moorings? Although that would upset as many people as much as the dearth of moorings does. The reasons people chose to live on boats are myriad. There are the leisure boaters who love the way of life and want to traverse the canal system but there are also those who live on boats because it is a cheaper alternative to bricks and mortar. And there are many who choose a boat rather than the alternative of homelessness: the divorced and dispossessed, the unemployed and erratically self-employed. Circumstances change even for those who regularly cruised; old age, mental issues and ill-health creep up. The C&RT recognise the problem and have appointed a social welfare officer to make contact with the more vulnerable boat residents. With escalating house prices, over-crowding on the canals in London and other expensive housing areas of the country can only get worse.

Once again I moor in Paddington Basin but this time it's a very brief stay. I'm reminiscing and resting here before starting the journey back to Northamptonshire where I first met Rea. It's the start of my last, long journey on her. The plan is to put the boat on brokerage when her licence expires at the end of June and it's now the beginning of April. Before she goes to the brokers she has to be out of the water for blacking and she needs some of the TLC that I have failed to give her over the last seven years. I'm not going to hurry along the Grand Union Canal I'm going to dawdle so I can savour this last journey on my beloved boat.

This time I'm going to enjoy working the locks instead of thinking what a hard task this is and how they slow my journey down. I'll enjoy talking to other boaters as we wait for the locks to fill, even when they're moaning about all the rule breakers on the canal system and the lack of maintenance by C&RT. I will love the long summer nights on quiet stretches of countryside and I'll relish the contrast of those quiet nights to the noisier ones when I'm moored outside a pub on a warm evening. I'm going to stop at the places I thought looked nice/interesting/strange when I passed on my previous journeys along the Grand Union. I will walk into Milton Keynes Centre (although I have no intention of shopping). I will stop at Bletchley and visit the Bletchley Park Museum. There are any number of pubs I thought looked worth a visit, maybe I'll stop at them all. I'll definitely re-visit the White Bear at Rickmansworth because I loved their curries. Hopefully I won't be there on their open-mic night when, on my last visit, the first two singers managed to empty a busy pub. If it takes me longer than three months to reach my destination then I'm happy with that.

Bob and dog are on board as I leave Paddington Basin but he allows me to take the tiller alone instead of, as is his usual habit, standing on the gunwales and chatting away as we amble along the waterways. He disappears to sit in the bow. The dog goes with him, both of them instinctively understand that I want this time alone with my boat.

The leaving of Paddington Basin is both sad and symbolic for me. It's not just that I came here as a single woman boater and enjoyed my time in Central London it was also that I was here for the more momentous events of my life during the last couple of years.

I reverse the boat out of the finger mooring and go down to the end of the basin where the circular fountain has now been completed and the water spurts from amongst the paving stones. The wind carries the spray across workers hurrying to the offices and against the windows of the M&S café. It always seems to be windy in Paddington Basin. I would have thought the high-rise buildings would shelter it but instead they seem to funnel the wind down towards the boats trying valiantly to turn in a small space at the end of the basin where a large audience of passers-by, residents in the blocks of flats and workers in the offices watch on.

On the finger mooring nearest to the bridge that curls open at noon every Friday a blue narrowboat sits. That was where I was moored when my daughter and her boyfriend came back from South America and had a coming home/engagement party at the Blacksmith and Toffee-maker pub in Clerkenwell. I thought that its lovely name reflected the historical connections of trade in Clerkenwell, but it turns out that the pub once had the ubiquitous name the Red Lion then after a number of changes it adopted the name of a Jake Thackeray song. When the party ended my sister and I caught the busy night bus home and staggered back to the boat. We were in no fit state to be allowed anywhere near water but somehow managed to negotiate the narrow finger pontoons and scramble on board safely.

On the last space in the basin where a wide-beam is now berthed I was moored last summer for two weeks. C&RT had given me permission to leave my boat there when my ex-husband and father of my children was taken ill and died.

I leave the basin. The drone of the generators at St Mary's Hospital, the clatter of wheels of the cases being dragged over the cobbles and the continuing noise of building work are just audible over the chunter of my engine. I go under the bridge passing through the aerated stretch of water which collects the urban detritus and prevents much of the rubbish from passing down into the smart new area of Paddington Basin. I once moored above this stream of aerated water but only for a few hours, the constant rumble of water under the boat was low but somehow disturbing. It seemed to reverberate through the boat penetrate my bones and churn away in my stomach. I soon headed off looking for a less disturbed mooring. As I head down the branch of the Arm back towards the main canal, a cold wind blows straight into my face. The book barge is still sitting at the exit to Paddington underground station. When the rental of the site went up for auction the Book Barge was outbid by British Land who own many of the developments around here. The Book Barge was told to move on. I, and sixty thousand other people, signed a petition to let it stay here. I know that C&RT need to realise as much income as possible from the rent of their sites but the character of the canals, about which they regularly proclaim, is enhanced by a quirky barge selling books and not by a large development company advertising their properties. I hope the Boat Barge can stay but I doubt it will.

Turning left into Little Venice I pass the café boat and move under the white arched bridge. Unusually there are no boats waiting at the water point and sanitary station and it feels a missed opportunity not to take advantage of a rare quiet period here but I just pass by without needing to stop to fill up or empty out. Although it is early the usual group of drinkers stand by the rubbish disposal area, Special Brew cans in hand chatting amiably to each other. It was here that I was moored when my daughter was married and again a year later when her son was born. I have memories of two lovely, happy days of wedding celebrations and of one very long night waiting for a call saying the baby had arrived and both mother and baby were well. I start to feel nostalgically tearful.

I head under the Harrow Road Bridge passed the seven-day moorings at Kensal Rise and the cemetery at Kensal Green. I was moored here on a few occasions on my passage in and out of London. I recollect being woken one morning by a clear, pure voice singing Amazing Grace to a small group of people gathered around a canal side grave. I always meant to go for a walk around Kensal Green Cemetery because I love the peace and beauty, the ornate headstones, the family tombs and the plethora of wildlife in Victorian cemeteries. I never did go. I shall just have to add it to the very long list of places I meant to visit but never did. Many of them are places I lived or worked near and knew that I could always go tomorrow but I moved away or changed jobs before that tomorrow arrived. Now I have a list of places that I should have visited when out on the canals but never did because I knew I'd be back again. This time I know I won't be back.

Once I have crossed the North Circular Aqueduct, looking down at the snarl of traffic underneath and being very grateful for being on the boat above instead of in a car below, I feel that I have left London. I know that once I've passed the green of Perivale Woods and the golf course that the industry of Northolt and Southall and the miles of unappealing towpaths and rubbish strewn water will appear. Then I will eventually turn right to reach the main arm of The Grand Union. I've still got a long journey ahead of me but this journey out of London has seemed like the end of another chapter of my life.

So why am I leaving and selling up? Circumstances have changed. My son-in-law has bought me out of the flat I part owned with my daughter in London and I decided I better buy a house before prices escalated and I found I could only afford a bed-sit in Scunthorpe. I have chosen to buy one in deepest Essex (but it is near the sea). To have space will be good so my son, daughter and their families can come to stay. To be static will be good so I can join in local activities and sign up for night classes and courses. To have more time will be good because moving a boat ten miles can take an awful lot of time: time that I can waste in so many other ways.

The sun comes out from behind blustery clouds and I feel a glow of warm spring sunlight on my face. As I wave to boats passing and greet boaters on the bankside, as I watch

314

the black rooks wheel noisily against white clouds and as I see the bright green buds of spring on the bushes along the towpath I do wonder if I have made the right decision. I will miss this simpler way of life: a life living without too many possessions. It's no good accumulating possessions because there's nowhere to keep them on a sixty-foot boat. I will miss the camaraderie of the waterways, having inconsequential chats with boaters on the towpaths and in the canal-side pubs. I will miss sharing locks with strangers and sharing journeys and histories for an afternoon then going our separate ways either to never meet again or to pass two years later and take the opportunity to renew a fleeting friendship. I will miss summer evenings on isolated moorings watching the sun go down and listening to the calls of the birds gradually fade as the water darkens. Then as the moon rises and slowly, almost imperceptibly, crosses the sky I will miss watching the silvery patterns form on dark water. I will miss listening to the boat creak into life on bright mornings as the sun warms the steel. I will miss being moored in the middle of large towns where a day's exploring or a night out only means a short walk before I'm back home in my city centre apartment.

Most of all I'll miss putting the kettle on for the first cup of coffee of the morning, opening the curtains and looking out onto water and wildlife.

I won't miss winter.